Hiking Trails of the

BOULDER

MOUNTAIN PARKS AND PLAINS

3RD EDITION

Hiking Trails of the

BOULDER

MOUNTAIN PARKS AND PLAINS

Vici De Haan

Contents

Preface

How many people realize the wealth of hiking trails that are available to them right here in our own back yard? As a native of Boulder, I have spent many glorious hours tromping through these foothills and would like to share my enjoyment of the out-of-doors with any others who also enjoy hiking.

All mountain trails included in this booklet were personally hiked by the writer during the 1976–1978 season. All open space trails were checked out in 1988. In checking out these areas, I found that many of them were hardly used at all and, at times, I was the only person on the trail. Perhaps a knowledge of other areas for hiking will help to decrease the number of people currently found on such popular trails as the Mesa Trail.

Since there are already some good trail guides available for hiking around East Portal, Fourth of July Campground, Brainard Lake, and Rocky Mountain Park, trails in these areas will not be included.

The aerial photos included in the booklet were taken by the writer from a private plane. I have found that sometimes it is difficult to visualize the area to be hiked from just looking at a topographical map; flying over the same area gives a much broader perspective.

Since this is a hiking booklet, no technical climbs will be included. The Boulder Public Library does have some good books available describing various rock climbs in the area.

There are some steeper climbs described in the booklet, such as to Mallory's Cave and up Fern Canyon, but none of these will require the use of technical equipment. However, you might find that "all fours" can be helpful at times.

Footwear is an important consideration on some of the steeper hikes, and particularly along the trails in the high country. Hiking boots offer better support than tennis shoes as well as providing protection from water.

Experience has shown that the "layering" method of dressing can be quite helpful. If the hiker begins with as much cotton next to the skin as possible, the hike will be much more comfortable.

Since the majority of the trails have little or no water available, the hiker would be well advised to carry a canteen, particularly during the hotter months.

Many of the hikes may be made as single hikes, or may be combined with other trails, making circular trips out of them. These trips are suggested in the booklet.

The question of timing for a particular hike is an individual matter. As a rule of thumb, it is better to allow too much time than to run the risk of having to grope your way back in the dark.

Acknowledgements

Special thanks go to Betty Reeves, Betty Lane, Buell Hamilton, Linda Light Bump of the Boulder County Open Space, Ralph Schell of Jefferson County Open Space, Brian Peck and Ann Wickman of the Boulder Mountain Parks, and to Ralph Johnson of the U.S. Forest Service for their assistance in finding new trails. I am also grateful to John and Adele Parmakian and Ray De Haan for looking over the original manuscript. Special thanks go to Warren De Haan for providing his services as a pilot to enable me to get the aerial shots.

Happy hiking!

October 1983:

Thanks to Rich Smith and Laurie Schwartz, Boulder park rangers, who took time to update me on the newest trails in the Boulder Mountain Parks and Open Space.

September 1988:

Thanks to Pat Reed and Randy Coombs from Boulder County Parks, and to Mark Gershman from Boulder City Parks for their extremely helpful assistance in updating the maps and providing information about the newest additions to our ever-expanding trails.

Since my time was very limited in doing this new revision, I am also thankful to Jayne Satter, Kathy Lanterman, and Paul Harris for their assistance in checking out the trails that I couldn't get to.

The Joy of Hiking
by
Vici De Haan

People often ask me why
I climb those mountains to the sky.
I would only reply:
        Have you ever
Walked through woods so deep and dark,
Along rushing streams cold and white,
Through fragrant meadows lush with flowers,
Up peaks with views unsurpassed
Or listened to the wind rustling through the trees
Or felt on your face the warmth of the sun
Or watched fluffy clouds that billow and float
Or smelled the forest after a rain
Or seen a deer bounding with alarm
Or flushed a ptarmigan that thought it was a rock
Or sat beside a mountain lake for lunch
Or shared your meal with a bumblebee
                        a camp robber
                        a chipmunk
                        a marmot
And been at total peace within your soul?
Then perhaps you too have known
The utter joy that a hike can bring.
        Happy hiking!

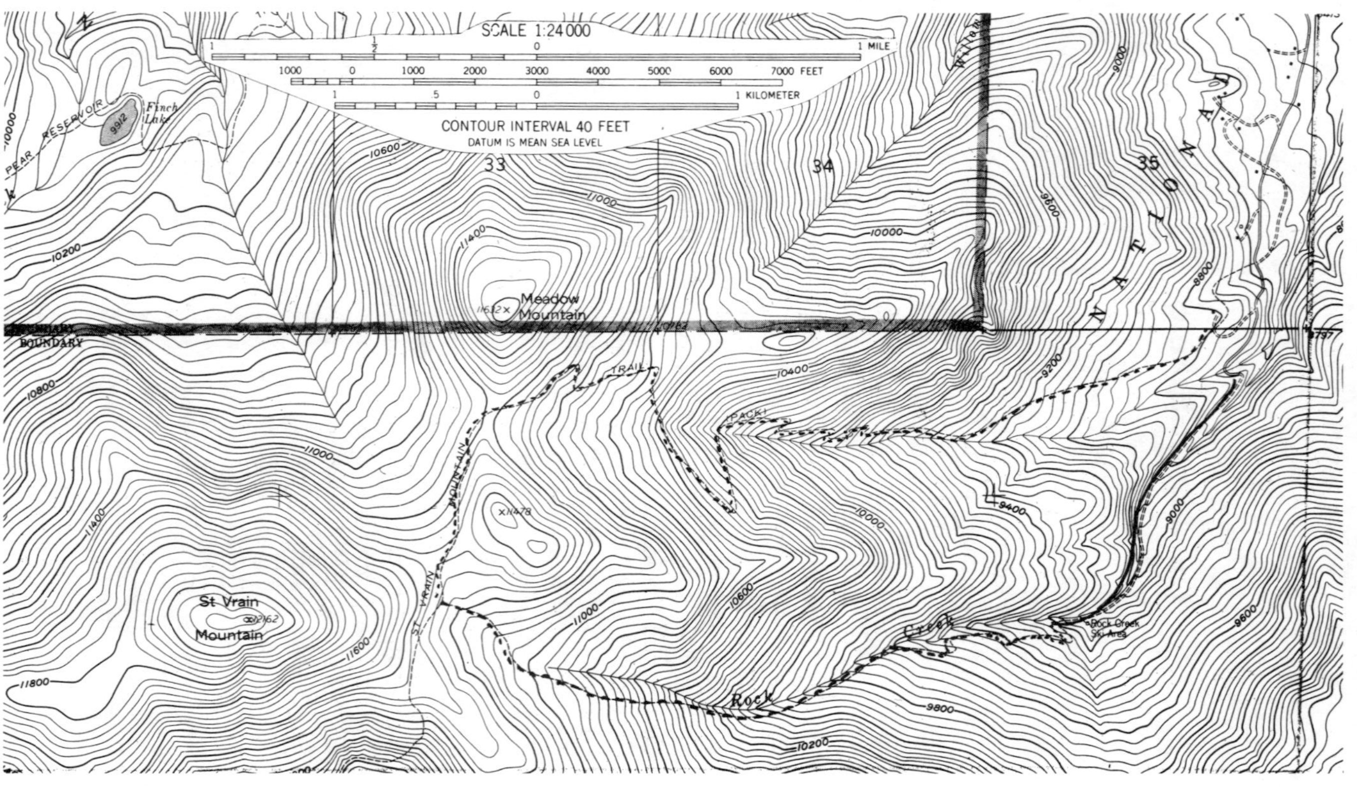

SCALE 1:24000
1 MILE
1000 0 1000 2000 3000 4000 5000 6000 7000 FEET
1 KILOMETER
CONTOUR INTERVAL 40 FEET
DATUM IS MEAN SEA LEVEL
33
34
35
NATIONAL
Willo
BOUNDARY
797
Finch Lake
RESERVOIR
PEAR
9912
Meadow Mountain
11612
St Vrain Mountain
11162
11478
TRAIL
PACK
ST. VRAIN MOUNTAIN
Rock Creek
Rock Creek Ski Area
9400

Allenspark Area

Meadow Mountain

St. Vrain Mountain

To reach these mountains, take Highway 36 to Lyons. From Lyons, take Highway 7 to Allenspark (20 miles). Turn left at the sign that indicates the Allenspark business area. Drive through Ferncliff and, after approximately 5 more miles, you will reach a dirt road heading south. The road has many signs on it, including two Ski Road signs. Turn left here and keep to the left at the next fork. After 1.8 miles, you reach another fork for the Meadow Mountain Trail. After .6 mile, you will reach a parking area for the trail. The signed trail goes through a beautiful forest to the southwest, and continues above timberline to below the summit of Meadow Mountain (11,630 feet). The trail doesn't take you to the top of the mountain itself, but since you are so high, you should have no difficulty selecting a good route up.

At timberline on the Meadow Mountain Trail

Allenspark: Once above timberline, beautiful relics of trees are visible on the skyline

To climb St. Vrain Mountain on the same day, return to the trailhead used to climb Meadow Mountain and follow it over to St. Vrain. Again you will have to choose your own route to the top. St. Vrain is 12,162 feet high.

Distance to Meadow Mountain: 4 miles one way
Elevation gain: 2,800 feet
Distance to St. Vrain: 5.5 miles one way
Additional elevation gain: 532 feet

Another option for climbing these peaks is to take the Rock Creek Ski Road to the camping area. From here, if you have a four-wheel-drive vehicle, you can go in a short distance before leaving your car. Intercept the St. Vrain Glacier Trail and proceed from this trail to the summit of each peak as before.

Sunshine Canyon

Bald Mountain Scenic Area

Bald Mountain is an area which is used quite frequently by the Boulder Mountain Park rangers who offer nature hikes in the area. To reach Bald Mountain, go up Sunshine Canyon 4.3 miles west of Memorial Hospital. Bald Mountain is on the south side of the road. The trail is very well marked, climbing about 200 feet.

Total round trip: 1 mile

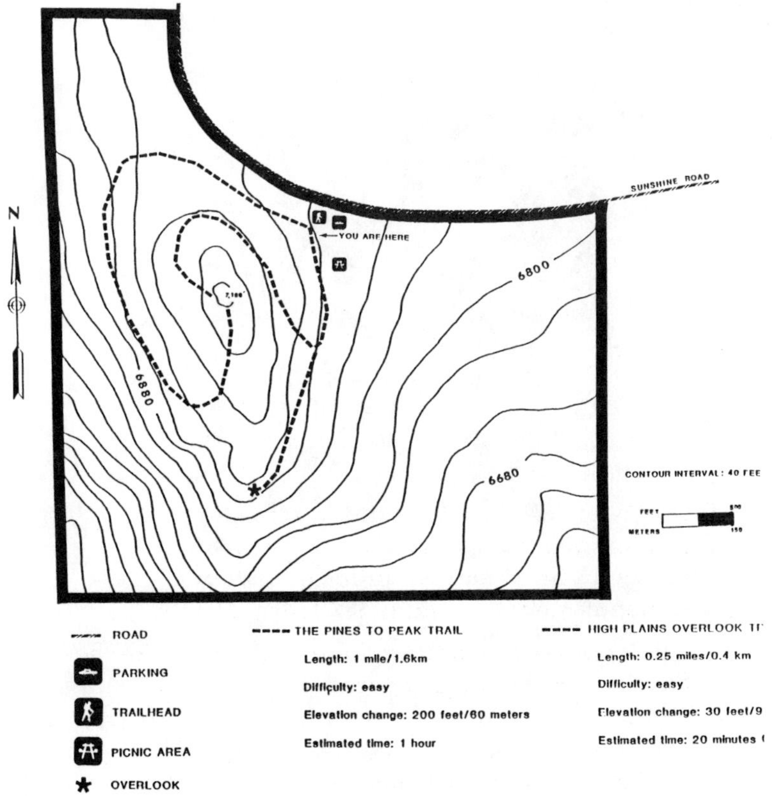

Bald Mountain: Sign at the entrance

Old wooden chute once used for loading
cattle around 1918 (Bald Mountain)

Betasso Preserve

Bummer's Rock

Canyon Trail

Bummer's Rock: The Betasso Preserve consists of 713 acres of forested land complete with some old mining equipment that might be of interest to mining buffs.

To reach the area, drive up Boulder Canyon to the Sugarloaf turn-off. Turn right and continue 1.3 miles, watching for the City of Boulder Water Treatment Plant sign. Turn right at the sign and go .4 mile to the Betasso Preserve.

To go to Bummer's Rock, don't turn into the area marked for the preserve, but stay on the main road for .1 mile. Watch for the concrete pad on the left-hand side of the road. A parking area is available directly opposite here with the unmarked trail to the rock which heads off to the south. It climbs through a beautiful pine forest and ends on some rocks that are fun to climb. The hiker also gets a good overlook of the canyons surrounding the preserve.

Distance: .5 mile
Elevation gained: 270 feet

Mining equipment found on Betasso Preserve

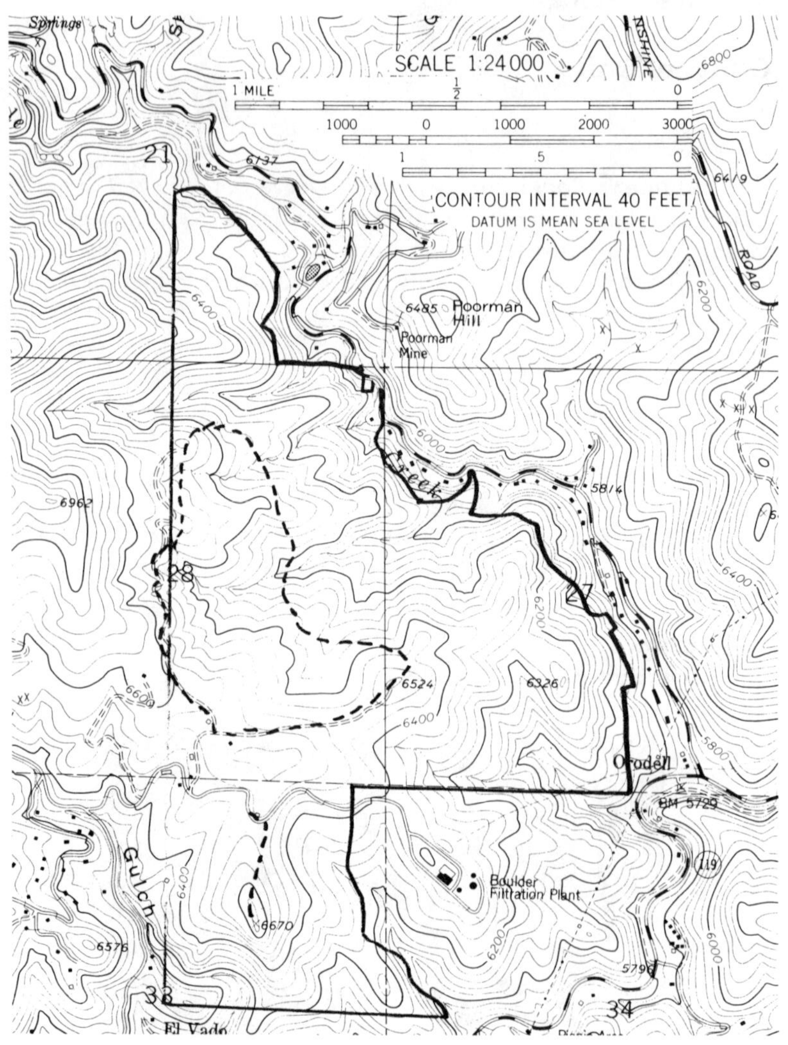

Springs
SCALE 1:24 000
1 MILE
1000   0   1000   2000   3000
CONTOUR INTERVAL 40 FEET
DATUM IS MEAN SEA LEVEL
21
6737
6800
64/9
ROAD
6400
6200
6485
Poorman Hill
Poorman Mine
6000
Creek
58/4
6962
6400
28
6524
6326
6200
6400
6602
6660
Orodell
BM 5729
119
Gulch
6049
Boulder Filtration Plant
6200
6670
6576
5790
6000
33
34
El Vado

Bummer's Rock

Old out-buildings near western end of Canyon Trail at Betasso

Canyon Trail: For a longer hike, turn into the preserve and drive in .4 mile. Park in the lot and hike down approximately 400 feet through the dense forest. Cross the stream and wind your way back up to your car. In 1988, the rangers were considering possible closure of the trail in the future because of the heavy erosion that is occurring.

Round trip: 2.9 miles
Elevation lost and regained: approximately 400 feet

Eastern end of Canyon Trail

Boulder Mountain Parks

The trails in the Boulder foothills offer a great variety of hiking possibilities. Beginning with the easy hikes such as the Mesa Trail, the area also includes some very steep areas such as Mallory Cave and Fern Canyon.

The trails in the park are clearly marked with color-coded hikers. A green hiker indicates an easy hike; yellow, a more difficult one; and red, the most difficult.

Although the area also contains many good technical climbs, these will not be included here.

The animal life in the park is quite diverse. If lucky, you may run across the large herd of deer that roam the mesa around NCAR, or see a fox just at dusk. There are many Abert squirrels in the forests, as well as many jays that let you know they are around. There are also marmot to be found, near the National Institute of Standards and Technology as well as on the southern end of the Mesa Trail.

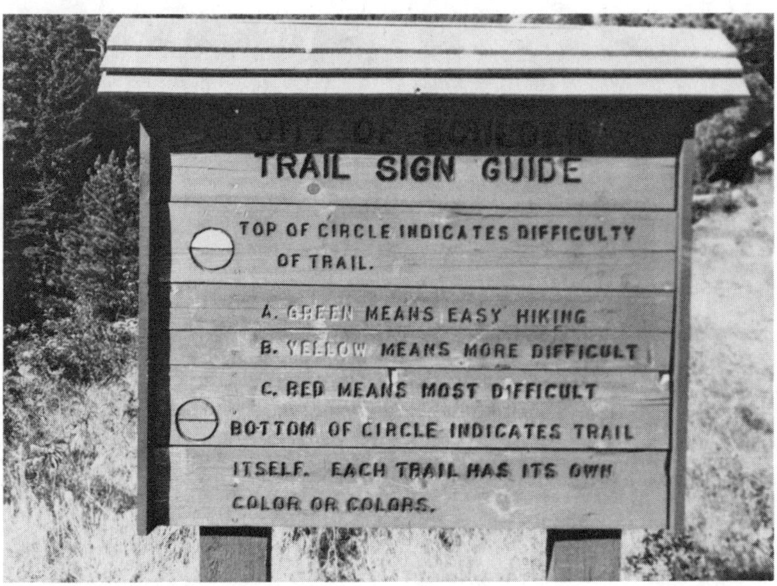

Sign guide for Boulder Mountain Parks trails

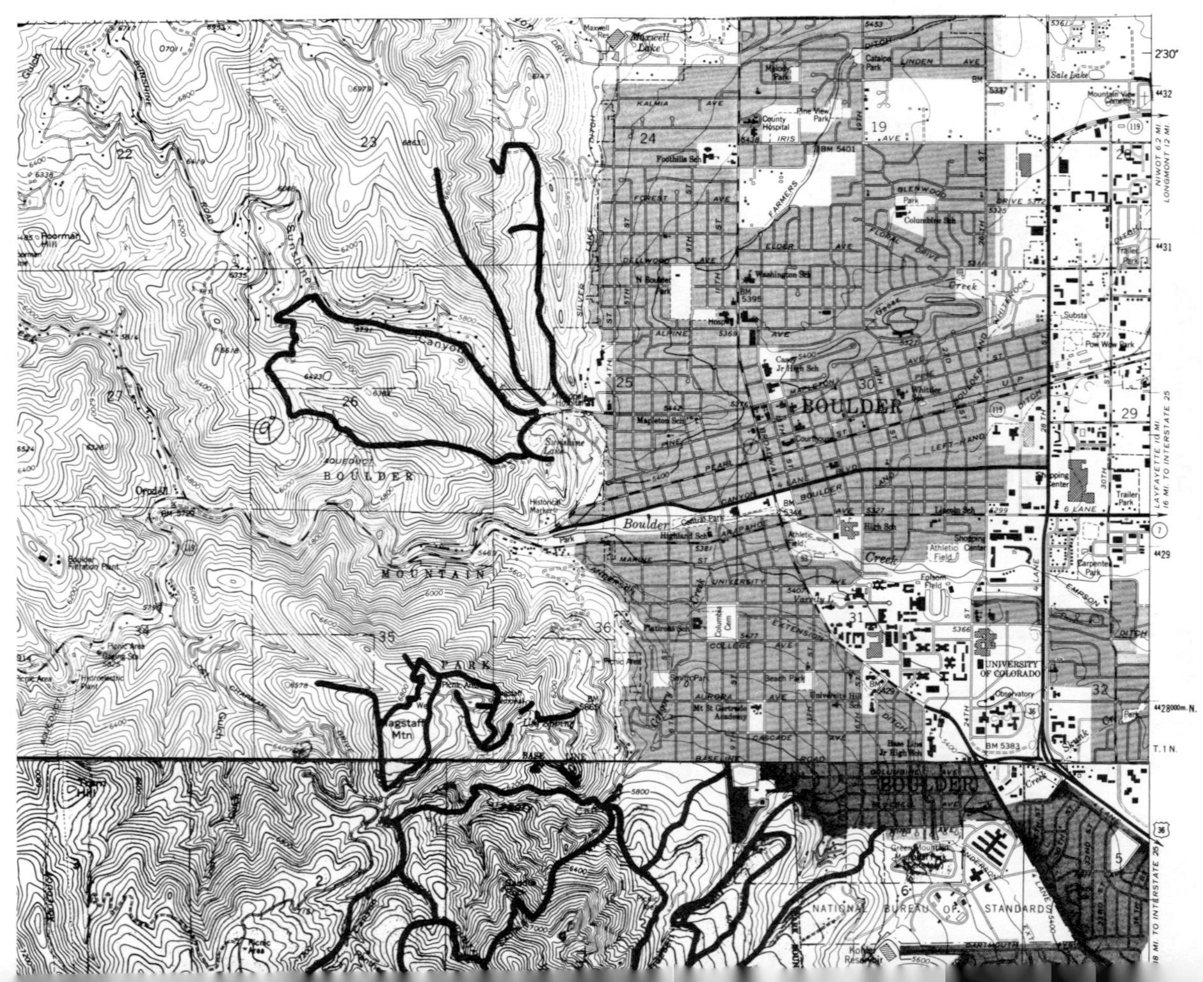

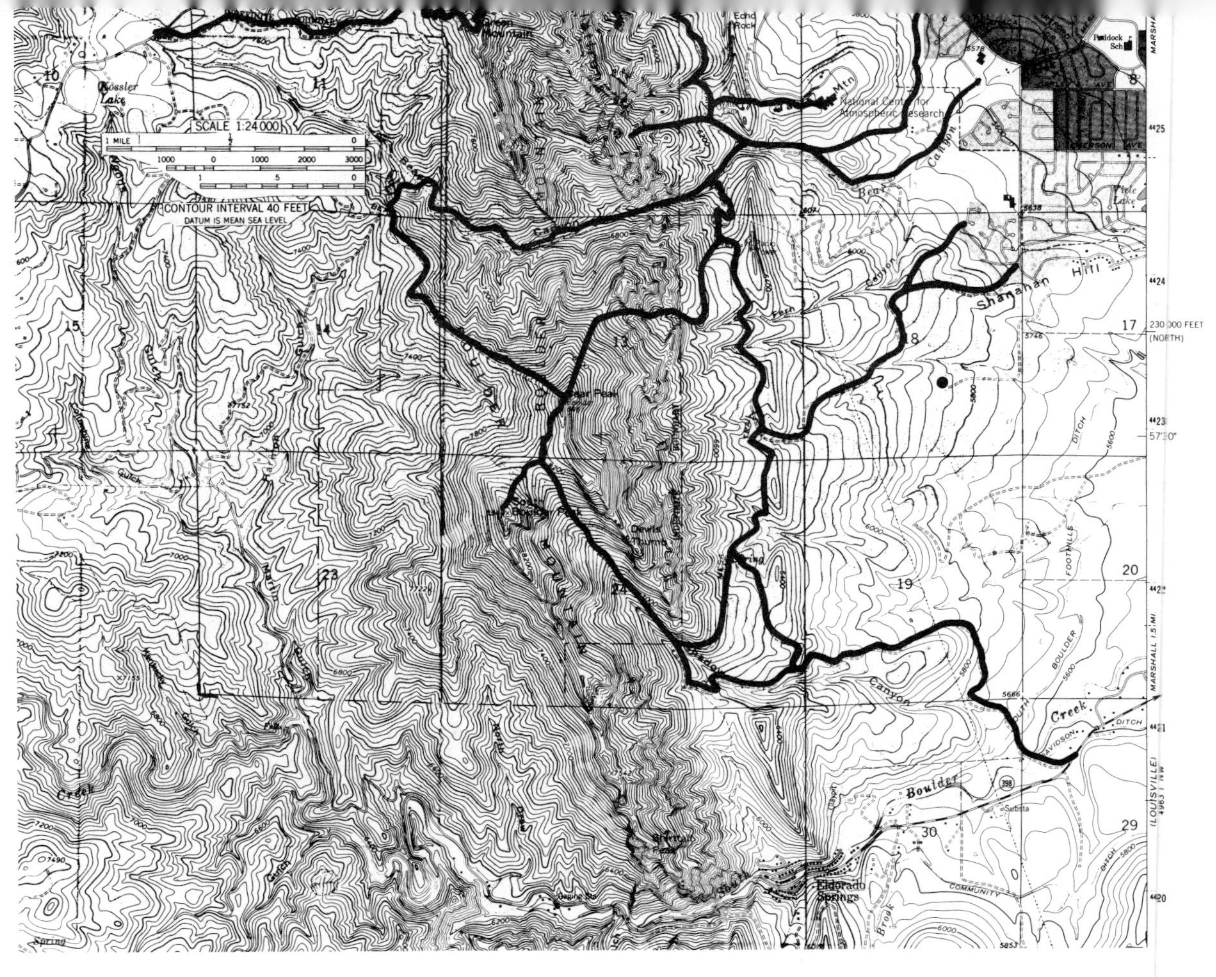

SCALE 1:24000
CONTOUR INTERVAL 40 FEET
DATUM IS MEAN SEA LEVEL
Eldorado Springs
Boulder Creek
Shanahan Hill
National Center for Atmospheric Research
Bössler Lake

11

The flowers along these trails are quite beautiful. The area offers a wide variety of blooms throughout the summer, making a hike along trails such as the Mesa Trail a real delight.

MESA TRAIL

Have you taken a walk through geological history lately? This can be done very easily by taking the Mesa Trail from Chautauqua to Eldorado Springs. The rock you see along this hike is the result of erosion from the ancestral Rockies which were located west of Boulder. The deposits have hardened into the sandstone which you see all about you.

The beginning of the southern end of the trail is often more exposed to the sun and therefore much hotter than the northern end, and many hikers prefer to start at the northern end, which begins just below the Bluebell Canyon Shelter House. However, if the group is large enough, you might wish to consider exchanging car keys with a group beginning at either end.

The trail leaving Chautauqua passes through a beautiful forest of ponderosa pine. There are a few Abert squirrels in these woods. They may easily be identified by their black or gray color, and

The NCAR Service Road comes up from the lower left, below NCAR. Bear Creek runs along the left side of the road, after coming down the center of Bear Canyon visible in the upper right hand side of the aerial.

12

Looking southward along the Flatirons. Green
Mountain is on the right. Bear Mountain and
South Boulder Peak are farther to the left.

pointed, tufted ears. The forest is also the home for many Steller's
jays which often screech at intruders.

About a mile from the start of the trail, the hiker has a good
viewing point of the familiar Flatirons as well as of the old Woods-
Bergheim rock quarry. A short distance farther to the south, you'll
pass a small stone cabin off to the west of you. This cabin is located
on a half acre of private land that is surrounded by the city-owned
land. It belongs to one of the original Boulder homesteaders and
is sometimes rented out during the winter. It should be cheap housing since it offers no gas, electricity, or running water. The trail
drops from here to cross Skunk Creek, then climbs to the meadow
just west of NCAR. The spring and summer flowers along this
meadow are quite spectacular.

Upon reaching the road, follow it to the west for a short distance, then turn south and cross Bear Creek. The road continues
uphill to the south for a short distance before turning west and then
south again. Just below the microwave tower, the trail leaves the
road to go south through more woods and to cross more meadows.

Upon reaching the next fire road, turn left to go to the southern
end of the Mesa Trail at the trailhead north of Eldorado Springs.
If you follow this fire road to the right, you will come to the mouth
of Shadow Canyon.

As you head southeast down the road, watch behind you for
the rock formations called the Matron and the Maiden, often
climbed by technical rock climbers. The cabin you pass part way

13

down the road and off to the south of you was built in 1903 by one of the Dunn's workers in exchange for his room and board in their household. The stone was carried to the site by a yoke of oxen and a cart.

As you approach Eldorado Springs, you get a good look at the Maiden and Devil's Thumb, both favorites for rock climbers.

Just before the end of the trail, watch for the marmots which often sun on the rocks, giving themselves away with their shrill cries.

The stone house known as the Dunn Cabin, located at the very end of the trailhead, was built in 1874–5 by John Debacker. He was one of the first families to homestead along South Boulder Creek during the 1860s. He raised chickens and cattle on the land. The Dunns bought the house in 1901 and lived there until 1953. The house, now padlocked, has one room downstairs and two upstairs, and is used by the Boulder Parks Department for storage purposes.

Distance one way: 6 miles
Elevation gain: 600 feet
Difficulty: Easy

Accesses to the Mesa Trail

1. Begin at Chautauqua (northern access).

2. Begin at the southern end located off Highway 170 just outside of Eldorado Springs, 1.6 miles west of Highway 93 (Rocky Flats Road).

3. The first trail that you encounter as you hike from the southern end of the Mesa Trail is the South Boulder Creek Trail. This trail begins from the City Open Space Operations Center located on Highway 93, 1.1 miles south of the intersection of Greenbriar and Broadway. It starts out on fairly level terrain, passing through several gates, before climbing gently to join the Mesa Trail.

Distance to the Mesa Trail: 2 miles
Elevation gain: 600 feet
Difficulty: Easy

4. Big Bluestem's trailhead also begins from Highway 93 by the South Boulder Creek Trailhead. It's reached by going west for .5 mile along the dirt road north of the South Boulder Creek parking lot. Big Bluestem eventually joins the Mesa Trail in two different places.

Distance from Highway 93 to first intersection: 2.3 miles
Distance to second intersection: .8 mile farther up the draw
Elevation gain: 600 feet
Difficulty: Easy

5. South Shanahan Trail begins in South Boulder from Hardscrabble, one block east of the Lafayette/Lehigh intersection. Turn right on Hardscrabble, heading south, and go to the end of the street.

Where the trail forks left after a few hundred yards, going to a water tank, take the fork to the right to climb through a beautiful forest. At the second fork, turn left to follow the fire road used for South Shanahan Trail.

Distance to the Mesa Trail: 1.9 miles
Elevation gain: 700 feet
Difficulty: Easy

6. North Shanahan Trail also begins from Hardscrabble. Upon reaching the second fork in the trail, stay to the right to climb up to the Mesa Trail.

This trail can also be reached from the Devil's Thumb subdivision by starting at the intersection of View Point and Briarwood streets. Go west into the cul-de-sac to park. You'll see an iron gate here where you should begin hiking up the hill to the southwest. Once you're up the hill and have entered the trees, you'll join the Shanahan Trail. Stay to the right to continue hiking up to join the Mesa Trail.

Distance: 1.3 miles
Elevation gain: 700 feet
Difficulty: Easy

7. The NCAR Trail begins west of the NCAR parking lot, reached by following Table Mesa Drive west to NCAR. Go around on the north side of the buildings, watching for the path that heads west. You'll drop down, and then climb one ridge before reaching the Mesa Trail.

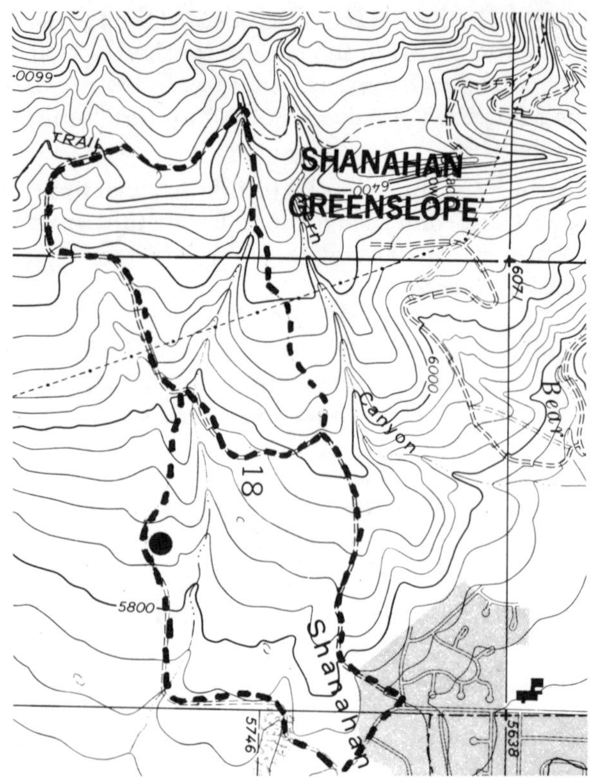

Distance to the Mesa Trail: .5 mile
Elevation loss: 80 feet
Difficulty: Easy

8. Park on Stoney Hill Road, reached by following Table Mesa Drive west to Lehigh. Turn south on Lehigh for one block, then west onto Bear Mountain Drive. Turn west again onto Stoney Hill Road. Park in the cul-de-sac at the end of this road and look for the trail that heads to the northwest. It crosses Bear Creek after a short distance and then links up with the NCAR Service Road. After approximately one mile, you'll intersect the Mesa Trail heading to the north. If you stay on the road, you'll cross Bear Creek and climb two more hills to rejoin the Mesa Trail as it heads to the south below the microwave tower.

Distance to first intersection of Mesa Trail: 1 mile
Elevation gain: 500 feet
Difficulty: Easy

9. Skunk Canyon Trail is reached by following Table Mesa Drive west until you reach the end of the houses. Watch for the paved bikepath off on the north side of the road. After a short distance, this path joins a dirt road. Follow this dirt road to the west, staying on the south side of the houses. When you reach the end of the road by the power substation, continue to the west, crossing over the bridge, and hike up to join the Mesa Trail. Caution: Watch for poison ivy on the west side of the bridge.

Distance: .7 mile
Elevation gain: 530 feet
Difficulty: Easy

10. The "People's Trail" also begins from Table Mesa on the west side of the houses. Park at the intersection of Vassar and Table Mesa Drive, and hike along the dirt track that heads to the south. After going down two hills, you can either turn right and head southwest up the trail that passes north of the power substation, or continue to follow the road, climbing through a fence, and hiking farther to the southwest. At the top of a short hill, this road curves to the west and heads up to the Mesa Trail.

Distance: 2 miles
Elevation gain: 500 feet
Difficulty: Easy

11. Four Pines Trail begins at 17th and King, south of Baseline Road. Hike up the hill, staying to the right where the trail forks, to join the Mesa Trail.

Distance: .5 mile
Elevation gain: 500 feet
Difficulty: Easy

12. The Enchanted Mesa Trail begins on the east side of the Chautauqua Theater. This trail is actually a fire road which goes to the south at first, before turning to the west, where it intersects the Mesa Trail.

Distance: 1.2 miles
Elevation gain: 400 feet
Difficulty: Easy

13. McClintock Nature Trail also begins behind the Chautauqua Theater. Drop down the east side of the paved road by the picnic area. The trail is level at first before beginning to climb, crossing a small stream. After you cross the fire road, it gets steeper. Watch for the signposts that point out various natural features to be seen in the area.

Distance: .6 mile
Elevation gain: 300 feet
Difficulty: Easy

14. The Bluebell-Baird Trail begins at the Baird parking lot, reached by driving west up Baseline Road to the base of Flagstaff Mountain. After crossing the stone bridge, turn left and drive west on the dirt road to the small parking area. If you park facing south, you'll be facing the trailhead, which crosses a small wooden bridge.

Leave the Amphitheater Trail after crossing the stream and turn to the east. You'll climb steadily up to a ridge as you hike to the south, and then cross below the First Flatiron. Gradually you'll drop down out of the trees to reach the Bluebell Shelter. To reach the Mesa Trail, go north of the shelter and head downhill to the northeast. The trailhead is clearly marked.

Distance: .8 mile
Elevation gain: 300 feet
Difficulty: Easy

15. The Chautauqua Trail begins at the entrance to Chautauqua Park on the west side of Bluebell Canyon Road. It climbs up through the meadow to join the Bluebell-Baird Trail. To reach the Mesa Trail, hike south on the Bluebell-Baird Trail.

Distance: .6 mile
Elevation gain: 280 feet
Difficulty: Easy

16. The newly established Bluebell-Mesa Trail begins southwest of the ranger station on the south side of the Bluebell Canyon Road. It provides access both to the Mesa Trail and the First and Second Flatirons.

Distance: .5 mile
Elevation gain: 300 feet
Difficulty: Easy

Accesses to the Flatirons

A new trail has been established that takes you to the First Flatiron. To reach it, hike up the Chautauqua Trail on the west side of Bluebell Canyon Road. This trail intersects Bluebell-Baird Trail after .6 mile. To reach the First Flatiron, turn right to hike about 25 feet, watching for the trail taking off to the west. It climbs steeply for between .25 and .5 mile to drop you at the base of the Flatiron.

Distance: .6 mile
Elevation gain: 800 feet
Difficulty: Easy

To reach the Second Flatiron, turn left on Bluebell-Baird Trail at its intersection with Chautauqua Trail. This trail begins a few hundred yards southwest of you, and is scheduled for completion in 1989. The part that is finished follows the contour of the mountain and comes to a talus slope where they've placed the rocks to form stairs. The trail continues on to the base of the Flatiron.

Distance: .5 mile
Elevation gain: 800 feet
Difficulty: Easy

In 1988, when I checked it out, it wasn't easy to find the trail when I returned through the talus, so keep track of other landmarks around you. Otherwise, you can return via other rougher trails that will take you back to the Bluebell Shelter.

Loop Hikes on the Mesa Trail

1. Begin at the south end of the Mesa Trail near Eldorado Springs. Follow the Mesa Trail to its intersection with the Shadow Canyon Trail (fire road continuation). Stay to the right on the Mesa Trail and climb to where another spur of the Mesa Trail comes in from the south. Turn left onto the trail and go south to intersect the fire road. To complete your loop, turn left onto the road and return to your car.

Distance for loop: approximately 3 miles

2. Park at 17th and King, south of Baseline Road. Follow Four Pines Trail uphill to the right to where it intercepts the Mesa Trail. Turn north and hike to the Enchanted Mesa Trail. Follow the

Enchanted Mesa Trail down to the east side of Chautauqua Theater. Stay on the right side of the road at this point so you can watch for an unmarked trail heading off down through the meadow opposite the theater next to the No Parking sign (1988). This trail will drop you onto Mariposa. Follow Mariposa east to 17th. Hike south 2 blocks to return to your car.

Distance: approximately 3 miles

3. Park at the Shanahan Trailhead on Hardscrabble off Lehigh in south Boulder. Hike up the North Fork of the Shanahan Trail to its intersection with the Mesa Trail. Turn south and hike to the South Fork of the Shanahan Trail. Follow this trail back to your car.

Distance for loop: approximately 3 miles

4. Another starting point for this same trail is from the Devil's Thumb Subdivision at the intersection of View Point and Briarwood streets. Go west into the cul-de-sac to park and hike through the gate, going southwest. A short distance after climbing the hill, this path will intersect the Shanahan Trail. Follow the North Shanahan Trail to its intersection with the South Shanahan Trail. Follow this second trail down. Once you have rejoined the North Fork Trail and are heading east, watch for the unmarked trail you came up in order to return to your car.

Distance: approximately 3 miles

5. Enchanted Mesa Trail: This trail, now widened into a fire road, is located near 12th and Mariposa where the road then swings behind the Chautauqua Theater. Park near the barrier and follow the road up to the city reservoir. The trail continues west from there, intersecting the Mesa Trail after 1.2 miles. Follow the Mesa Trail to its north end. Hike down the Bluebell Canyon Road to Chautauqua. Turn southwest to hike back to the theater and your car.

Distance: approximately 3 miles

6. McClintock Nature Trail: This trail starts at the west end of Mariposa and swings around east, staying below the Chautauqua Theater. The trail climbs gently up, crossing a small stream, to intersect the road leading to the Enchanted Mesa Trail. After crossing the road, it continues steeply up in a southerly direction to where it meets the Mesa Trail. It has some good markers describing

some of the natural features of the area. To finish the loop, turn south on the Mesa Trail and hike to the Enchanted Mesa Trail. Follow this trail down to your car.

Distance: approximately 2.5 miles

Another option for this loop is to hike north on the Mesa Trail and hike down the Bluebell Canyon road to Chautauqua. Hike back up to the theater to your car.

7. Park at Table Mesa and Vassar. Hike west on the bikepath located on the north side of NCAR. Continue hiking west, passing the houses on the north side of the trail. Soon you'll reach a power substation. Cross the bridge to the west, watching for the poison ivy, and continue up this trail until you reach the Mesa Trail. Upon reaching it, you have a couple of options.

a. Hike to the south until you intersect the road used to service the microwave tower. Turn east and hike down the road. When you see the road forking to the southeast by an old fence, follow the trail on the left side of you, heading uphill and then downhill to where you'll intersect another trail that runs along the west side of the houses. Turn north, hiking up two short hills to return to your car.

Distance: approximately 4.5 miles

b. Hike south along the Mesa Trail until you reach either the North Fork or the South Fork of the Shanahan Trail. Follow either of these downhill into Devil's Thumb, watching for the cutoff trail on the left just above the subdivision and shortly after the North and South forks merge.

Once in Devil's Thumb, follow View Point to Bear Mountain Drive. Turn left on Wildwood Road, watching for an access to a trail on the west side of the street next to 1195 Wildwood. This unmarked path leads to the dirt trail that goes uphill to the north and back to your parking spot.

Distance: approximately 5 miles

8. Park at Table Mesa and Vassar. Hike up the Skunk Creek Trail. Upon reaching the Mesa Trail, turn north and hike to the Four Pines Trail. Hike down this trail to 17th and King. For a longer loop, hike down King to National Institute of Standards and Technology (NIST). Turn right onto Compton Road. At the south

end of the cemetery on the west side of N₁ST, watch for a bikepath
heading southwest. Follow it uphill until you reach Foxtail Court.
Turn left and hike up the next hill to Hollyberry Lane. Then hike
to the east until you reach another short paved bikepath. Follow
this bikepath east to return to your car.

Distance: approximately 5 miles

For a slightly shorter loop, when you reach 17th and King,
take the trail that connects Four Pines at its beginning but heads
to the southwest up the hill. Follow this trail to its intersection with
the bikepath southwest of NIST and then proceed as described in
the longer loop.

9. Hike up Big Bluestem from its trailhead on Highway 93.
Upon reaching the Mesa Trail, turn south until you intercept the
South Boulder Creek Trail. Return via this trail to your car.

Distance: approximately 4.5 miles

10. For a round trip in the southern part of town, take Table
Mesa Drive west to Lehigh. Turn south for one block and then turn
west onto Bear Mountain Drive. Proceed west to Stoney Hill Road.
Park in the cul-de-sac and pick up the trail going northwest. Cross
Bear Creek and pick up the NCAR Service Road. Follow this road
west, then south as it crosses Bear Creek again. Stay with the road
as it bends west and then south until you are just below the microwave tower. Distance this far is approximately 2 miles.

Pick up the Mesa Trail and continue to hike for approximately
one mile, watching for the Shanahan Trail which intersects the
Mesa Trail from the east. Now to complete the trip, follow the
Shanahan Trail back out.

The best access to your car is to watch for where the trail is
just about out of the trees and you can begin to see the houses
in the Devil's Thumb Subdivision. There is a trail here that heads
northeast from the Shanahan Trail which will drop you down to
the intersection of Briarwood and View Point Road. Follow View
Point Road to Bear Mountain Drive and then on to Stoney Hill to
retrieve your car.

Should you miss this cutoff to Devil's Thumb, the Shanahan
Trail continues out to Hardscrabble. To return to your car, hike
north out Hardscrabble to Lehigh. Turn left and follow Lehigh to

Briarwood. Turn left and follow Briarwood to View Point Road. Turn right. This road will now lead you back to Stoney Hill Road.

Total round trip: approximately 5 miles

Chautauqua Round Trips

1. Go up Chautauqua Trail from the bottom of the meadow in Chautauqua Park to where it intersects the Bluebell-Baird Trail. Proceed along this trail until reaching the Bluebell Shelter House. From here, stay to the left of the shelter and head first north and then west along the paved road to the Mesa Trail's northern entrance.

To head back to your parked car at Chautauqua, either follow the Mesa Trail to the McClintock Nature Trail and down, or continue farther along the Mesa Trail until reaching the Enchanted Mesa Trail. This trail ends behind the Chautauqua Theater. Continue north along the paved road until past the theater, then cross to the west across the grass to retrieve your car.

2. Park in Baird Park. Take the Amphitheater Trail for a very short distance, watching for a fork off to the left, heading east. Now you are on the Bluebell-Baird Trail which will take you to the Bluebell Shelter House. From here you can take the road back down to the bottom of Chautauqua and then pick up the trail that crosses to the west along the bottom of the meadow, taking you back to your car in Baird Park.

Total distance: approximately 5.3 miles

Cave Hikes from the Mesa Trail: Mallory Cave, Bear Cave, and Harmon Cave

Mallory Cave: This is the largest cave known in the park, and is one of the most difficult hikes. A fast access to the trail leading to the cave would be to take the NCAR Trail west of the NCAR buildings to where it intersects the Mesa Trail. Turn south for a short distance, watching for the Mallory Cave trailhead marker off to the west.

The climb to the cave from the trail involves a good rock scramble of about 30 feet, but this trail is one which affords a tremendous view of the Flatirons and their uplifted rocks as well as a good overlook of the city.

Distance one way: .4 mile
Elevation gain: 700 feet
Difficulty: Most difficult

Mallory Cave

Large rock slab located beside the trail
to Bear Cave

Bear Cave is on the right

Bear Cave: This is a very small cave, but for those who enjoy visiting caves, it might be worth the time to find it.

Go up the Bear Canyon Trail which is reached by first going west on the NCAR Trail and turning south onto the Mesa Trail. Continue to follow the Mesa Trail as it joins the NCAR Service Road. The road heads west, then south crossing Bear Creek, and then west once again. Upon reaching the top of the next hill and heading west, watch for the large power antenna and a trail marker for Bear Canyon.

Follow this trail west for about a quarter of a mile. Watch for a large rock slab and a place along the hillside to your right where others have scrambled down to the creek. It's marked with three steel posts in the ground below the trail. After the trail descends to cross Bear Creek, it then involves a steep scramble up the hillside north of the creek for about .25 mile. The cave does have a faint resemblance to a small black bear.

Harmon Cave: This is a medium-sized cave located just off the Mesa Trail. To reach it, take the Mesa Trail to its intersection with Bear Canyon, as described in the Bear Cave hike. Continue uphill to the south for a short distance after passing the Bear Canyon Trail,

Harmon Cave

watching carefully on the upper hillside for an unmarked trail heading off to your right to the west.

When you spot the faint trail, you'll see that the bank you'll have to scramble up to reach it is quite steep, so you may wish to proceed farther up the road a short distance to climb up the bank and then return to the trail.

The trail climbs steeply between two talus slopes of rock for approximately .25 mile. The cave is clearly visible off to your right as you come out into a small meadow. Boulder Mountain Parks would probably rate this spur as one of their most difficult hikes since it's quite steep.

Distance from Mesa Trail: approximately .5 mile

Royal Arch

This is truly a "heads up" hike, because the trail markers have been posted along the trees, and when climbing the steeper section, your eyes will more than likely be down.

The hike begins south of the Bluebell Shelter House near the picnic table that is just off the road.

The trail itself is steep, ranked as an intermediate hike. It climbs first on the west side and then on the east side of Bluebell

Looking south through the arch

Canyon. Upon reaching the saddle, you get two good views. One looks out over Boulder to the southeast and, by going a few feet to the right of the rocks on the saddle, you get a good look at the arch itself.

Watch for a sign posted by the Colorado Mountain Club at the saddle, for it is easy to get off onto a false trail here. From the saddle, the trail descends about 80 feet before climbing back up between some gateway rocks. The last stretch climbs south until you arrive at the natural sandstone arch affording the climber a well-won view of Boulder and another of the Flatirons.

Distance: 5 mile round trip
Elevation gain: 1,200 feet
Difficulty: More difficult

Bear Peak Via Bear Canyon and Bear Canyon West Ridge

Bear Peak, located on the southern side of the Flatirons, is a very beautiful climb. Once on top, the climber can truly see the full effect of the beetles that effectively killed the majority of the trees on the western slopes.

To begin the hike, park at NCAR. Take the NCAR Trail until it meets the Mesa Trail, where you will continue south to the intersection of the Mesa Trail and the NCAR Service Road. This road goes west a short distance, then turns south to cross Bear Creek. It then climbs uphill to the south before turning west again. At the top of this hill, watch for the power substation located on a trail which heads to the west, while the road portion of the Mesa Trail continues to the south. The Bear Canyon trailhead is by this power station and has been marked by a Boulder Mountain Parks signpost.

Follow this trail west for 1.5 miles, climbing 900 feet and crossing Bear Creek several times. Just before reaching the West Ridge Trail, you will climb up a steep hill. Once you drop down the other side of this hill, watch for the trail which crosses Bear Creek once more and heads to the south. Follow the Bear Peak West Ridge Trail until reaching the west ridge of the peak. From here, head southeast to where you will have a good scramble through the talus and boulders found just below the summit.

Distance one way to the summit: 3.2 miles
Elevation gain: approximately 2,200 feet
Difficulty: More difficult to peak
Most difficult up peak

Bear Canyon's beginning as it leaves the NCAR Road

Uptilted sandstone rocks
along Bear Canyon

One of the many good views
of the Flatirons as seen from
the Bear Canyon Trail

Bear Peak Via Fern Canyon

This is one of the steepest accesses to the peak, and is often used as a descent. The Boulder Parks Department rates this as one of their most difficult hikes.

To reach the Fern Canyon trailhead, you can take the NCAR Service Road. To reach it, drive west on Table Mesa Drive to Lehigh. Turn south for one block on Lehigh, and then west onto Bear Mountain Drive. Follow this street to Stoney Hill Road. Park in the cul-de-sac at the end of this road and watch for the trail which heads northwest. It crosses Bear Creek after a short distance and then links up with the NCAR Service Road.

Follow the service road to the west, turning south to cross Bear Creek. Stay with the road as it turns south; just below the micro-wave tower, you should begin watching for the trail sign posted on the right, a short distance below the Mesa Trail turn off.

At first the trail climbs steeply to the southwest. Just below the large rock slab on the north side of the trail, you will find the many ferns that gave this trail its name. Near the large slab, watch for Fern Spring, marked by an old metal marker on a tree. Stay with the trail heading straight up and to the west.

Once you reach the saddle located between Nebel Horn and Bear Peak, climb to the southwest, staying on the ridge. This leads you into some talus which makes the climbing of Bear Peak a good challenge, but one which has its own rewards.

One of Bear Canyon's
steeper sections

Fern Canyon distance one way: 1.3 miles
Distance from NCAR Road to summit: 3.5 miles
Elevation gain via Fern to summit: 2,100 feet
Difficulty: Most difficult

Fern Canyon Trail just before
the going gets tough

A rock slab visible along
Fern Canyon

South Boulder Peak Via Shadow Canyon

The easiest access for this peak, joined to Bear Peak by a saddle, is from the southern entrance to the Mesa Trail off Highway 170. Travel up the trail for two miles, following it to the Stockton cabin. This cabin is located at the end of the road.

Cross the small pond to the west of the cabin and pick up the Shadow Canyon Trail which heads straight up in a westerly direction. On the way, you will pass two favorites for rock climbers: Devil's Thumb and the Maiden.

Once you reach the shoulder, you can decide which peak you wish to climb first. In order to climb South Boulder Peak, watch for a faint trail going to the southwest which ends up in some very large boulders. From here you have a scramble to the summit and a tremendous view of the mountains to the west.

South Boulder Peak is 8,550 feet.
Distance one way: 3.6 miles
Elevation gain: 2,700 feet
Difficulty (both hikes): More difficult

DeBacker cabin along the southern end of the Mesa Trail

Stockton cabin just
below the beginning
of Shadow Canyon

Shadow Canyon signpost

View of the Maiden, clearly visible from Shadow Canyon

Bear Peak

There is no marked trail for climbing Bear Peak. From this same shoulder at the top of Shadow Canyon, turn to the north. Be sure to stay on about the same elevation but on the west side of the mountain. You will wind through the forest to a talus slope. At this point you should also meet the Bear Peak West Ridge Trail. Take this trail to the summit.

Bear Peak is 8,461 feet.
Distance one way: 3.7 miles from Mesa Trail
Elevation gain: 2,700 feet
Difficulty: More difficult

South Boulder or Bear Peak Round Trip

A two-car shuttle is necessary for this one. Leave one car in the NCAR parking lot. Drive the other car to begin from the southern entrance to the Mesa Trail, and take the Shadow Canyon Trail up to either peak. To climb both in one day, first climb South Boulder Peak, and then drop back to the saddle and climb up Bear Peak.

There are now two options for returning to your car. You can pick up the Bear Peak West Ridge Trail which will take you back to Bear Canyon. From there, pick up the Mesa Trail and follow it back to the NCAR Trail and back to your car.

Another possibility is to leave Bear Peak via the Fern Canyon Trail. This trail also brings you to the Mesa Trail just a short distance south of Bear Canyon. The return to your car is then about the same as for the first option.

Distance up South Boulder-Bear Peak via Shadow Canyon and returning via Bear Peak West Ridge: approximately 9 miles

Distance up South Boulder-Bear Peak via Shadow Canyon and returning via Fern Canyon: approximately 7 miles

Difficulty: More difficult; up Bear Peak: Most difficult

South Boulder Peak–Bear Peak: Shadow Canyon splits the two peaks on the left-hand side of the picture. Fern Canyon, with its rock slab on the north side of the trail, is also visible.

Flagstaff

Anyone traveling west on Baseline Road can see the flagpole that is on top of Flagstaff Mountain. In order to reach the summit on foot, drive over the stone bridge that is on Baseline Road as it turns north up Flagstaff. Right after crossing the bridge, watch for a dirt road which leads to Baird Park, and which is off to the west. Park at the intersection of Baird Park Road and Baseline Road, for the trailhead is off to the north of here.

The trail climbs steeply to the northwest before gradually leveling off to cross through some beautiful shrubs and flowers. Then the trail begins to climb steadily up to the first crossing of Flagstaff Road. You will cross this road four times, with each crossing marked by painted lines along the road. However, the last time you cross the road, you will need to walk to your right or to the east for a few hundred yards to get back onto the trail. It is located in a pull-out area on the northeast side of the road.

While you are on this last and steepest stretch, you can easily reach the flagpole by taking the last right-hand spur, or the Plains Overlook Trail, which leads you to the lookout. Otherwise, by continuing on with the Flagstaff Trail, you will once again reach Flagstaff Road near the overlook on top.

Flagstaff Road is visible climbing the mountain on the left side of the photo. Boulder Canyon winds its way up in the foreground.

Once on the top of Flagstaff, you'll see a summit house on your right close to the amphitheater. It's open on weekends during the summer. There's also water in a nearby tank which is kept filled for summer visitors.

Distance: 1.5 miles
Elevation gain: 1,050 feet
Difficulty: More difficult

Flagpole on the summit of Flagstaff

Additional Flagstaff Mountain Trails

Boy Scout Trail and May's Point: One end of this trail begins at the northeast corner of the Sunrise Circle Amphitheater located on the top of Flagstaff and off to the south of the overlook parking area. The trail comes out by the picnic area on the northwest side of the mountain.

To pick up the trail from the picnic area, take the road from the summit to the northwest for a short distance. Park by the picnic table and take the trail going downhill to the west. After approximately .3 mile, there is another path that takes off to the west to May's Point, but which is unmarked. The Boy Scout Trail continues to the east at this intersection, ending up at the amphitheater. There are some good overlooks of Mount Sanitas along this walk.

Distance one way: .6 mile
Elevation gain: 80 feet
Difficulty (Boy Scout): More difficult
Difficulty (May's Point): Easy

Boy Scout Trail as it
comes off Flagstaff

Tenderfoot Trail: Begin at Realization Point and the picnic
area on the northeast side of the road. Realization Point is located
about three-fourths of the way to the top of Flagstaff Mountain
where Flagstaff Road turns back to the east and the Kossler Lake
Road continues to the west. The trail heads north for about a mile
before intersecting an old road going to the west. After going down
for a short distance, this old road heads uphill quite steeply. From
the top of this hill, the road continues off to the south. However,
since this road leads to a road on private property, permission
should be obtained before taking it. The road ends up in Boulder
Canyon.

Distance one way: 1.5 miles
Elevation gain: 1,000 feet
Difficulty: More difficult

Ute Trail: This trail has two possible starting points along the
top of Flagstaff. The southern trail may be picked up by crossing
Flagstaff Road and turning to the southwest after you climb the
stone stairs by an old well. The trail heads downhill on the west
side of the mountain and ends up at Realization Point.

Tenderfoot Trail junction with Range View at
Realization Point

Tenderfoot Trail

Ute Trail as it climbs on the south side of Flagstaff

The northwest trail begins from the Range View Trail which starts behind the shelter house on Flagstaff, and it is well marked at its beginning with many stones. Watch for the Ute Trail; it takes off to the right and goes downhill steeply. After a short distance, it meets the Boy Scout Trail.

Distance one way on southwest trail: .5 mile
Elevation gain from Realization Point: 160 feet
Difficulty: Easy

Plains Overlook: This short trail may be picked up in two places. First, you can begin at the Sunrise Circle Amphitheater on the south side of the lookout on Flagstaff Mountain. Here you take the first right-hand trail that goes west.

The other access is from the Flagstaff Trail, just a short distance before it meets Flagstaff Road. The Plains Overlook Trail takes off to the northeast and gives a beautiful overlook of the plains to the east.

Distance one way: .3 mile
Elevation gain: 40 feet
Difficulty: Easy

Range View Trail: This is another trail on the top of Flagstaff. To find its beginning, proceed west of the shelter house on the northwest side of the mountain. The trail is well marked with stones, and winds around the shoulder of Flagstaff, affording a tremendous view of the flat top of Longs Peak off to the northwest, of Audubon

Range View Trail offers
good views of the
mountains to the west

with its giant "crater" left behind by a glacier, and of Arapaho Glacier, one of Boulder's sources of water. The trail ends up at Realization Point.

Distance one way: .5 mile
Elevation gain: 160 feet
Difficulty: More difficult

Gregory Canyon: When hiking this trail uphill, and crossing some of the rocky areas, it is hard to imagine that this was once part of the old stage road going to Magnolia. The trail begins at the west end of the Baird parking lot. Head west through some beautiful shrubbery, particularly during the fall, and climb uphill until you meet the road that continues west to the Green Mountain Lodge.

Distance one way: 1.2 miles
Elevation gain: 800 feet
Difficulty: More difficult

Gregory Canyon's rocky trail was once an old stage road

Circle Trips on Flagstaff: To go up, take the Flagstaff Trail all the way to the road that comes up to the top. Then head northwest behind the shelter house to intercept the Range View Trail. This trail will take you to below the very top of Flagstaff, and circles the mountain, eventually dropping onto the west side of the mountain at Realization Point.

When you reach the picnic table at Realization Point, cross the road going to Kossler Lake and pick up the dirt road going downhill to the southwest. Stay to your right at the first switchback. This fire road will then go west, heading for the Green Mountain Shelter. At the next intersection, you leave the road to go downhill to the east until you come to the green tank. Here turn to the south, crossing the creek, and pick up the Gregory Canyon Trail which will return you to your car.

For a slight variation on this, stay with the Flagstaff Trail as for the above hike. Then, instead of picking up the Range View Trail, pick up the Ute Trail on the southwest side of Flagstaff and follow this trail down to Realization Point. Then once again pick up the Gregory Canyon Trail and continue back to your car.

Round trip: approximately 4 miles

Green Mountain

Green Mountain is one of those must hikes in the Boulder Parks. If lucky, the hiker might just be on top at the same time a glider decides to ride the winds that provide lift for it.

There are several routes that can be taken to the summit.

Gregory Canyon — Saddle Rock — H.L. Greenman: To reach the Gregory Canyon Trailhead which is located at the bottom of Flagstaff Mountain at Baird Park, drive into the Baird Park parking area located west of the bridge where Flagstaff Road turns north. Park here and head south of the Boulder Parks sign which is posted directly west of the parking lot. Cross over the bridge that takes you to the Saddle Rock/Amphitheater Trail. You climb south at first before turning west. The trail is 1.2 miles long and climbs 1,200 feet.

This trail will then continue to the southwest to connect with the H.L. Greenman Trail. This trail will take you to the summit of Green Mountain. The Greenman Trail is 1.5 miles long with an elevation gain of 1,500 feet.

Distance one way up Green Mountain: 3.2 miles
Elevation gain: 2,700 feet
Difficulty (all four trails): More difficult

One of Saddle Rock's less steep sections

Saddle Rock Trail at its intersection with Greenman Trail

Amphitheater Trailhead

Amphitheater: a rock climber's favorite

Gregory Canyon — Ranger Trail: Another option is to take Gregory Canyon to the Green Mountain Shelter House. Then, instead of taking the H.L. Greenman Trail, continue to follow the Ranger Trail when it forks right until it intersects the Green Mountain West Ridge Trail which will take you to the summit.

**Distance one way: 5.0 miles
Elevation gain: 2,850 feet
Difficulty: More difficult**

Along the lower portion of the Ranger Trail, there is an interesting side trip that may be made to an old cabin. To get there, watch for a little-traveled trail a few hundred yards off to the left and just above the Green Mountain Shelter House.

Green Mountain Shelter

Ranger Trail — Green Mountain West Ridge or H.L. Greenman (starting from Realization Point): A shorter hike up Green Mountain is to drive to the point on Flagstaff Road where this road turns east and Kossler Lake Road continues to the west. Park here and follow the fire road to the Green Mountain Shelter. Here you have the option of taking either the left fork up H.L. Greenman Trail to the top or remaining with the Ranger Trail to its intersection with the Green Mountain West Ridge Trail and then on to the summit.

**Distance via Greenman Trail: 1.5 miles
Elevation gain: 1,500 feet
Difficulty: More difficult**

**Distance via Ranger — Green Mountain West Ridge:
  2.3 miles
Elevation gain: 1,450 feet
Difficulty: More difficult**

The views from the top of Green Mountain include some of
the state's 14,000-foot peaks: Longs, Evans, and Bierstadt; as well
as some peaks over 13,000 feet: Arapaho, Meeker, and Audubon.
Watch for the stone cairn on the top of the mountain with its circular plaque that points out some of the various peaks along the
Continental Divide. There is also a registration canister for hikers
to sign which is located within this rock cairn.

Long Canyon

This is a beautifully wooded trail which can be reached from
Realization Point. Begin on the fire road going southwest, passing
the fire gate and keeping to the right when another branch of the
road heads east. Continue to the Green Mountain Shelter House,
where you go north around the house, crossing a bridge. The trail
then goes west from here. The trail comes out on the Kossler Lake
Road. From here, the hiker can go up the road .4 mile and catch
the Green Mountain West Ridge Trail to continue on to the summit
of Green Mountain.

**Distance one way: 2.5 miles
Elevation gain: 1,350 feet
Difficulty: More difficult**

For those willing to follow a trail that is rather faint but which
offers a quiet woodsy hike, there is another trail which intersects
the Long Canyon Trail and eventually winds its way through the
woods until it also meets the Green Mountain West Ridge Trail without having to follow the Kossler Lake Road.

To find this trail, located at the western end of the Long
Canyon Trail, and just before you walk out of the woods onto the
road, bear to your left and watch for a trail heading west and then
south. The trail contours around on the east side of the ridge before
crossing over to the next ridge where the trail runs south, running
into a fence. The West Ridge Green Mountain Trail can then be
intercepted from here.

Long Canyon Trail as it leaves Flagstaff Road

Entrance to the Green Mountain West Ridge Trail

Green Mountain West Ridge

This is one of the quickest accesses to Green Mountain as well as being one of the shortest. To reach the trailhead, take Flagstaff Road up and continue past the turnoff to Flagstaff's summit, continuing west towards Kossler Lake. From 6th and Baseline, the trailhead is approximately 4.7 miles up the road, and is located on the south or left-hand side of the road. It is marked with a Boulder Parks trail sign. There is also a chain across the road which serves as the trailhead.

This trail is well marked by double yellow Boulder Parks signs on its lower portion. The upper part of the trail was recently (1983) vastly improved and is now quite easy to follow. As you near the top of the mountain, watch for some wild raspberries in late August.

Distance one way from Flagstaff Road: 1.5 miles
Elevation gain: 600 feet
Difficulty: More difficult

Marker at summit of Green Mountain

Green Mountain Circle Trips

1. Go up Gregory Canyon Trail to the Range View Trail. From here, intersect the Ranger Trail and then the Greenman Trail heading for Green Mountain's summit. Return via the Saddle Rock Trail. Note: watch for this trail off to your right after you come down the steepest section of the Greenman Trail. It's been marked by a Boulder Mountain Parks sign.

Round trip: approximately 5.7 miles

2. Go up Gregory Canyon to the Ranger Trail behind the Green Mountain Shelter House and stay with this trail until it meets with the Green Mountain West Ridge Trail. Return via the Greenman-Ranger and Gregory Canyon trails.

Total distance: approximately 5.8 miles

3. Begin at Realization Point. Go up Long Canyon to the right of the Green Mountain Shelter House. Follow the Kossler Lake Road for .4 mile, watching for the West Ridge of the Green Mountain Trail. Return via the Greenman Trail.

Distance: approximately 4.4 miles

One of the twin springs on Green Mountain

North Boulder Trails

Mount Sanitas

Mount Sanitas Valley Trail

Red Rocks

Aqueduct Trail

Centennial Park Round Trip

Mount Sanitas: The trailhead is located just west of Memorial Hospital at 4th and Mapleton in North Boulder. Proceed just behind the hospital for approximately .25 mile and watch for the Knollwood Subdivision sign. The parking area for Mount Sanitas is north of this area on the north side of the road.

This is a steep climb with much loose rock, making the wearing of hiking boots advisable. Beginning from the parking area, head north for a short distance, watching for the trail going west and

Mount Sanitas trail marker

Uptilted sandstone slabs along Sanitas

uphill. The trail is well marked; it goes to the south of the ridge, and then it heads northwesterly to the top. Upon reaching the summit, you will find a metal pole cemented onto one of the rocks. At this location, there are some good overlooks of both the city to the east as well as of the mountains to the west.

Distance one way: 1.2 miles
Elevation gain: 1,200 feet
Difficulty: More difficult

Mount Sanitas Valley Trail: This road is located directly west of Memorial Hospital on the north side of the road. This is a jogger's delight, since it climbs very gradually up to some rock quarries.

Go around the fire barrier to head north. After approximately .75 mile, the first road turning left leads to a rock quarry. Continuing on the road to the north, the hiker will pass through a good-sized prairie dog colony. The road then bends to the west and climbs up to another rock quarry.

Distance one way to top rock quarry: approximately
   1.5 miles
Elevation gain: 200 feet
Difficulty: Easy

A twisted tree still stands along the Sanitas Trail

Much sandstone was once quarried from this area

One of the many prairie dogs that live along
the Fire Road

Red Rocks Park: Centennial Foothills Park has some beautiful
hikes available to both the rock scrambler and to anyone who just
likes to get up onto a high piece of ground to look out over the
city as well as towards the Continental Divide.

The access to the park is reached by driving west up Mapleton
toward Memorial Hospital. From the intersection of Mapleton and
4th, the trailhead is located .3 mile west and on the left-hand side
of the road. A parking area is located here.

Should you decide to do some rock scrambling, follow the
trail going south and watch for another trail turning off to the east,
going up to the uptilted rocks.

Red Rocks was where the first white settlers of Boulder established a camp on October 17, 1858. A story is told about a wagon
that was attacked by a band of Indians who massacred the family
aboard with the exception of a 13-year-old girl. She escaped and
hid in the rocks, but was found by one of the Indians and also shot
with an arrow. Her initials are reportedly carved on the rocks near
the site.

Distance: .5 mile one way
Elevation gain: 400 feet
Difficulty: More difficult

Red Rocks Park: These
sandstone rocks have many
cracks and crevices and even
some small caves to explore.

A rock scrambler looks for
another route at Red Rocks

Aqueduct Trail: If the hiker prefers something more challenging in distance, take the road as it heads to the south, and watch for a very steep climb off to the west. Here the original ascent is quite steep, but once it levels out, the hiker has some very gentle, rolling hilltops to walk along. The trail that follows the ridge intersects the road just at the top of its steepest part, heading off to the northwest. If you happen to miss the trail, you can bushwhack west up to the first ridge and find it. The trail then leads across three other ridges with very little altitude gain or loss until it comes to an end on a ridge that is south of the Mount Sanitas ridge.

From here, the hiker can either follow the trail back down to the west or retrace original footsteps.

There is some beautiful smoky quartz as you go up the road, easily visible because the trail is quite steep and your head is usually down.

Distance: approximately 2 miles one way
Elevation gain: approximately 400 feet
Difficulty: Easy

Centennial Park Round Trip: Begin in Foothills Centennial Park. Take the trail heading southwest along the Sunshine Canyon Road until you reach the end of an old barbed wire fence. Follow the fence uphill to catch the trail again. This trail gradually winds its way up to the top of a ridge. Once on top, take the fork to your left, heading east. This trail goes around the north side of the mountain, crossing the top of the ridge a couple of times. Whenever the trail seems to be dim, stay on the north side of the ridge and it will soon become apparent again.

Total round trip: approximately 3 miles
Difficulty: Easy

Eldora Ski Area Trails

Guinn Mountain

Bryan Mountain

Loop Hike

Guinn and Bryan mountains: To reach the trailhead, take Boulder Canyon to Nederland and continue through Nederland on Highway 119 to the southwest. Turn north onto the Lake Eldora road after 1 mile. You will then reach a fork in the road after 1.5 miles. Here you take the left turn for Lake Eldora. The ski area is approximately 21 miles from Boulder.

Park in the ski lot only if you know that you can retrieve your car by 4:30 p.m., because the gate will be locked at that time. If in doubt about your return, you can park just outside the gate.

There are four possible routes up Bryan and Guinn mountains:

1. The most direct route up Bryan Mountain is from the ski lodge. From here you can hike up the Cannonball ski run just west of the lodge. At the top of this hill, look for the ski-area road that continues off to the west, and after leaving the area, continues on to the shoulder of Bryan Mountain which is 10,796 feet. From this point, it is only a short distance to the summit.

Bryan is a good above-timberline hike which gives the hiker a good 360° view of the surrounding terrain.

Distance one way to Bryan: approximately 2.5 miles
Elevation gain: 1,523 feet

To reach Guinn Mountain, continue along the old pipeline roadcut for another 1.5 miles. Leave the road to hike to the summit of Guinn.

Distance from Lake Eldora one way: 4 miles
Additional elevation gain: 284 feet

2. Park in the southeast corner of the parking lot of the ski area. Going around the east side of the ticket booth, pick up the 17th Avenue ski-touring trail. After 1 mile, you reach an intersec-

Lake Eldora ski area. Starting at the top left, you can see the pipeline road which leads to below Guinn and Bryan mountains. Photo also shows the hiker why to avoid coming down the ski run in the back of the ski area.

Snow-covered stump in the winter along Jenny Creek

tion with Dead Man's Gulch Trail. Turn west here and continue down the hill into Jenny Creek Meadow. Stay on the road on the north side of the meadow, keeping Jenny Creek on your left. After approximately 3 miles, you will cross a tributary creek (which is often quite high in the early summer), and the road now begins to climb above Jenny Creek.

Turn right as the trail forks and now the trail becomes steeper. After about 1.5 miles, you will come to a three-way intersection. Stay left and follow the red-flagged road. Once you reach the clearing on the shoulder of the mountain, you will see a metal building. To reach Guinn Mountain Hut, maintained by the Colorado Mountain Club, continue west another few hundred feet. The hut is located on the south side of Guinn Mountain.

To climb Guinn, it might be easiest to turn north at the metal building and pick up the old pipeline road. After a short distance, you can easily see the summit of the mountain (11,080 feet) off to the west, and you can make your own way up.

Distance: 5.2 miles one way
Elevation gain: 1,850 feet

Guinn Mountain Hut in March

3. To climb Guinn from the ski lodge, begin on the service road that is located southeast of the lodge and runs beside a small pond. This road curves back to the east toward the bunny slope before gradually going up to the service road going out of the area. This pipeline road will take the hiker along the ridge between the two mountains.

To climb Bryan, bushwhack to the east. To climb Guinn Mountain, bushwhack up the mountain to the west.

4. Forest access to Jenny Creek and Guinn Mountain: Park in the lower lot by the ski ticket building. Then instead of taking the 17th Avenue touring trail to the east, stay to the west and climb the hill beside the Ho Hum chairlift.

Once on top of this hill, cross behind and south of the lift and follow the Foxtail ski trail until just below the steep hill or the Upper Bunnyfair ski trail.

Here watch for the forest-access signs as well as ski-touring signs. This access trail parallels the ski trail for a few hundred yards before taking off to the southwest and later to the west until it drops down the mountain ridge into Jenny Creek.

Once on the Jenny Creek trail, continue to Guinn Mountain as described above.

Loop Hike: For a loop, begin with the trail by the ticket office in the southeast part of the ski area, taking Jenny Creek up to Guinn Mountain. From there, continue along the pipeline road to Bryan Mountain. This road will then take you back into the ski area. At this point, be sure to continue along the road to the east, since the first ski run you come to will dump you onto the wrong side of the mountain from your car.

Round trip: approximately 9 miles

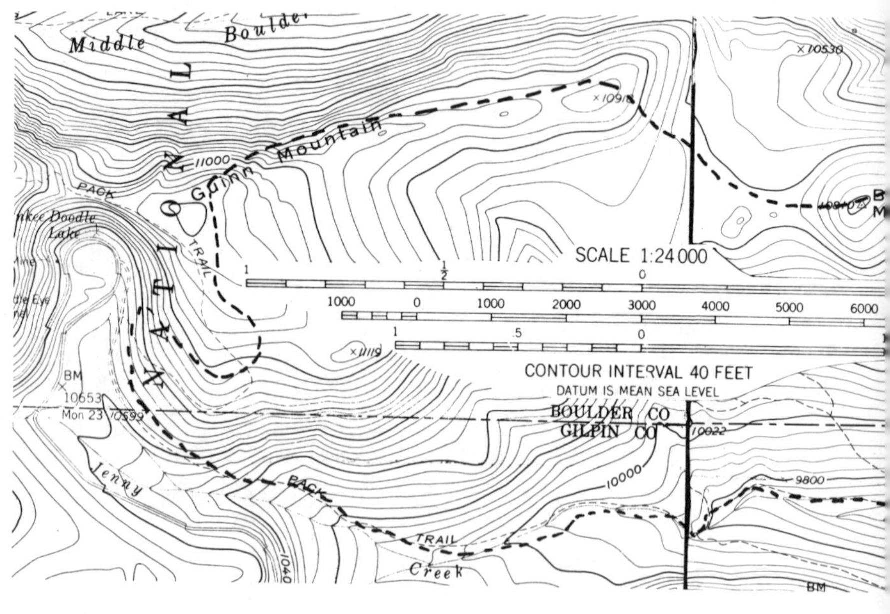

Middle
Boulder
×10530
×10918
Mountain
Gunn
11000
PACK
nkee Doodle
Lake
SCALE 1:24 000
1
1/2
0
le Eye
1000
0
1000
2000
3000
4000
5000
6000
×11119
1
.5
0
BM
×
10653
CONTOUR INTERVAL 40 FEET
DATUM IS MEAN SEA LEVEL
Mon 23
10599
BOULDER CO
GILPIN CO
10022
Jenny
10000
9800
PACK
TRAIL
1040
Creek
BM

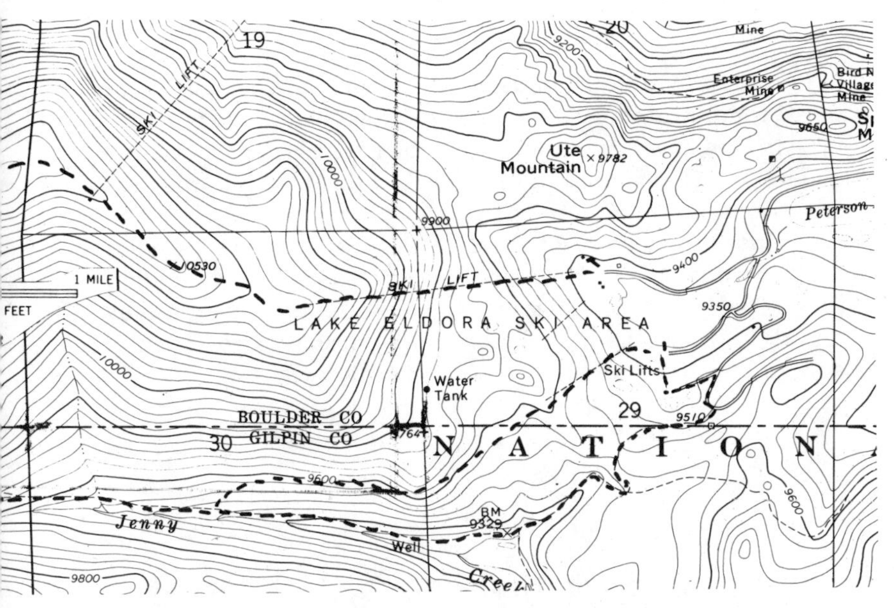

19
20
Mine
Enterprise Mine
Bird N Village Mine
SKI LIFT
9200
Ute Mountain
× 9782
9650
S M
Peterson
9900
10000
9400
10530
9350
1 MILE
SKI LIFT
FEET
LAKE ELDORA SKI AREA
10000
Water Tank
Ski Lifts
BOULDER CO
GILPIN CO
29
9510
30
9764
N A T I O N
9600
9600
Jenny
BM 9329
Well
Creek
9800

Town of Eldora

Eldorado Mountain

Mineral Mountain

Caribou Hill

Klondike Mountain

Spencer Mountain

Eldorado Mountain, Mineral Mountain, Caribou Hill, and Klondike Mountain: Have you ever come out of the woods at sunset just in time to watch the sun's rays color the blowing snow from the Continental Divide? If not, try hiking this trail just after the first snowfall in the high country.

The peaks may be climbed out of the town of Eldora, 24 miles west of Boulder. Take Highway 119 to Nederland, continuing through Nederland for one mile to the Lake Eldora turn-off. Stay to the right where the Lake Eldora Road turns left. The town of Eldora is approximately four miles from Highway 119.

Aerial shows the Lake Eldora ski area in the upper left. To the right is the ridge of mountains including Eldorado, Mineral, and Caribou.

Trailer at the beginning of Eldorado Mountain

Upon reaching the town, go to the center to the street where the Log Cabin Grocery is on the northeast side. Turn right here, going north for two blocks, passing the Gold Miner Hotel off to the west. Turn right (east) for one more block and park here along the street. Walk north for one more block, watching for a large white trailer on the northeast side of the road, and turn to the east. This jeep road travels east, then turns west to cross just below Eldorado Mountain at 9,660 feet. The road then continues through

Looking west from Eldorado Mountain Trail toward Lake Eldora ski area

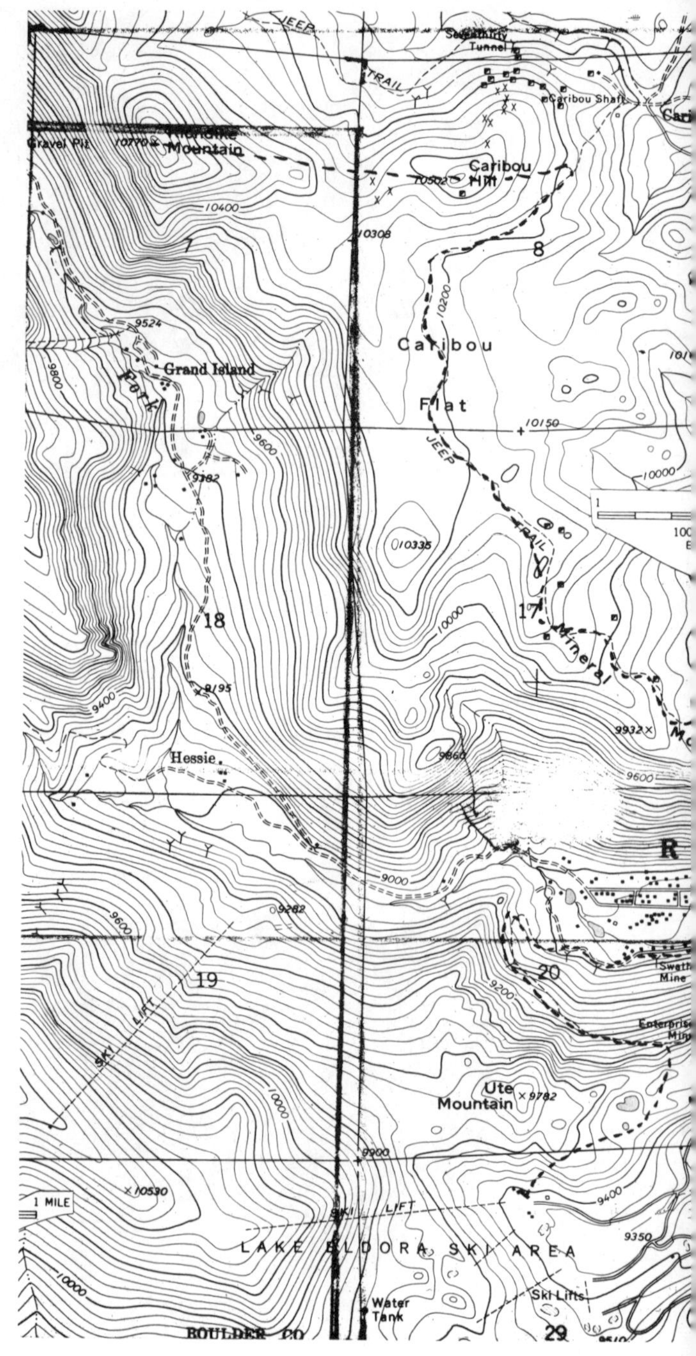

JEEP
Sugar Thirty
Tunnel
TRAIL
Caribou Shaft
Car
Gravel Pit
10770
Mountain
Caribou
Hill
10502
10400
10308
8
10200
Caribou
9524
Flat
Grand Island
9800
Fork
10150
JEEP
9600
9782
TRAIL
10000
100
E
10335
10000
17
Mineral
18
9932
9195
9860
9600
Hessie
R
9000
9282
9600
Swath
Mine
20
19
9200
SKI LIFT
Enterprise
Mine
10000
Ute
9782
Mountain
9900
1 MILE
10530
9400
SKI LIFT
9350
LAKE ELDORA SKI AREA
10000
Ski Lifts
Water
Tank
BOULDER CO
29

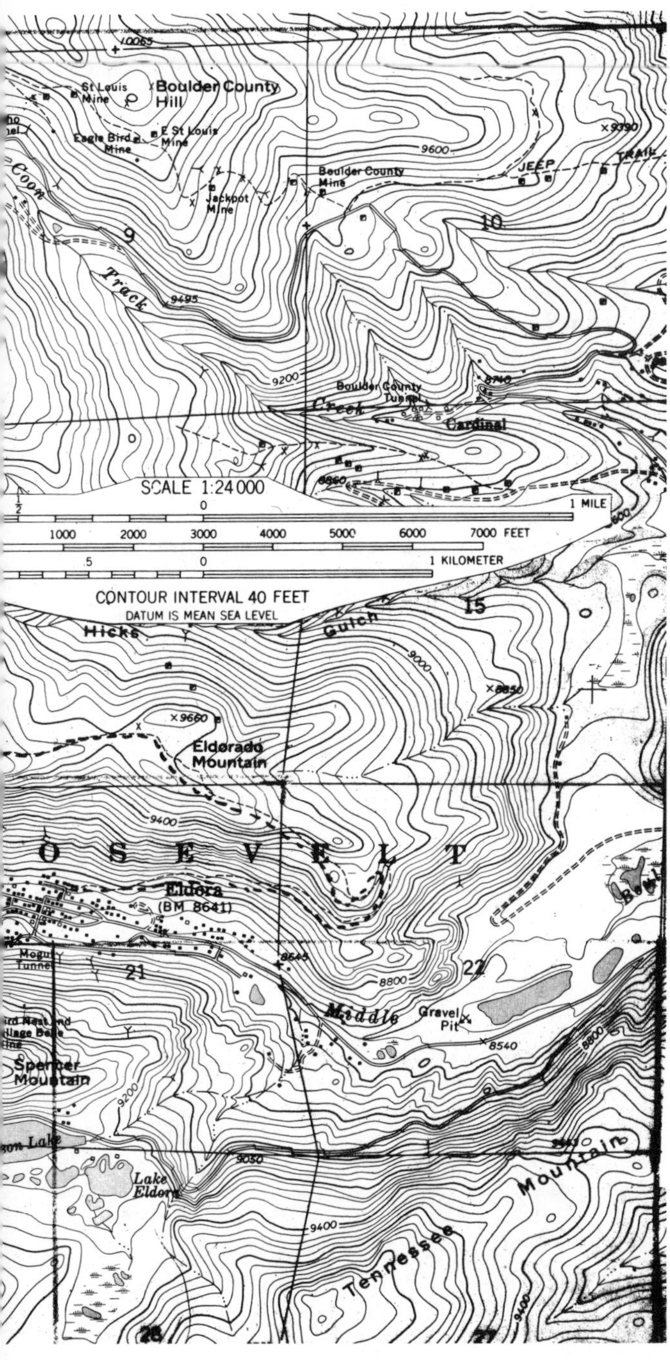

St Louis Mine
Boulder County Hill
Eagle Bird Mine
E St Louis Mine
Jackpot Mine
Boulder County Mine
JEEP TRAIL
×9390
9600
9495
9200
Track
Coon
Boulder County Tunnel
8740
Creek
Cardinal
8860
9
10
SCALE 1:24 000
0
1 MILE
1000 2000 3000 4000 5000 6000 7000 FEET
.5
0
1 KILOMETER
CONTOUR INTERVAL 40 FEET
DATUM IS MEAN SEA LEVEL
Hicks
Gulch
15
9000
×8850
×9660
Eldorado Mountain
OSEVELT
9400
Eldora
(BM 8641)
Mogul Tunnel
21
8645
22
8800
Middle
Gravel Pit
×8540
8800
Bird Nest and Village Belle Mine
Spencer Mountain
9200
Lake Eldora
9050
9400
Tennessee Mountain
28
27
9400

a beautiful forest to just below the summit of Mineral Mountain (9,932 feet). From here it goes north to cross Caribou Flat and west of Caribou Hill.

From here, there is no trail, but since you are now above timberline, you can easily see the path to follow to climb Caribou Hill (10,502 feet). From Caribou Hill, drop down about 100 feet, and then climb an additional 370 feet to make Klondike Mountain (10,770 feet).

Elevation gain from Eldora to Mineral Mountain: 1,291 feet
Elevation gain from Eldora to Caribou: 1,861 feet
Elevation gain from Eldora to Klondike: 2,129 feet

Spencer Mountain: For a shorter, scenic hike past a mine and over the ridge for a good look at the Lake Eldora ski area, turn south in the center of town where The Hitchin' Post is on the northwest corner of the street. Drive in along this road to the south and west for about .5 mile to where you will reach a clearing for parking a couple of cars.

From this point, the road climbs through a forest to curve around Spencer Mountain (9,639 feet). Upon reaching the three forks in the road, keep to the left each time.

The road continues on to descend into the northeast side of the Lake Eldora parking lot.

Round trip distance: approximately 4 miles
Elevation gain: 800 feet
Elevation loss: 200 feet

Jasper Lake–King Lake Loop

This is a very strenuous, but fantastically beautiful hike for those with great endurance. You have the option of either visiting three mountain lakes in one loop, or taking a longer hike involving more elevation gain and visiting all eight lakes in the area. Either choice is quite rewarding.

Since Corona Pass is below one of the busiest air routes in the area, there undoubtedly will be many planes to witness your climbing feat.

To reach the trailhead, take Highway 119 to the Eldora turnoff southwest of Nederland. Drive 1.5 miles and keep to the right, as the Lake Eldora road forks left. Continue on through the town of Eldora and onto a dirt road. Keep to the left upon reaching the fork for the 4th of July road. After about a mile, you will reach a small parking area near the old town site of Hesse.

This section of the road leading from the turnoff into Hesse is extremely rough and rocky and is often under water, so caution

View shows King Lake in the foreground. Skyscraper Reservoir is the other large lake located to the right. The Continental Divide section of the trail, shown on the left side of the picture, shows the hiker more clearly that he needs to stay along the ridge until passing the second cirque before starting down to King Lake.

Cabin below Jasper Lake

should be exercised. Many hikers prefer to park and walk this section.

From here continue to the west on foot along the old jeep road, crossing a bridge over North Fork Creek. Continue climbing, passing the turn-off to Lost Lake. After approximately .2 mile from here, you cross a bridge to the right to reach the fork for King Lake and Jasper Lake. Follow the trail to the right for 4.2 miles to Jasper

Jasper Lake

Lake. This lake has a concrete spillway which you will cross.

Continue to the west on to Devil's Thumb Lake (.8 mile). From here, continue to follow the trail as it goes west, climbing steeply up to the Continental Divide. This divide walk is exceptionally beautiful in the fall since there are several springs on top making the tundra quite lush.

Continue hiking south along the top of the Divide for about 3 miles, watching for the Corona Pass Road. This road is also called the Rawlins Pass Road. As soon as you can see the remains of the old restaurant-hotel on top of the pass, begin looking for the trail heading northeast back down into the valley to King Lake. The trail bypasses King Lake, and continues back to the original trail fork.

Round trip: approximately 15 miles
Elevation gain: approximately 3,000 feet

Devil's Thumb Lake

Jasper Lake
Devils Thumb
Devils Thumb Lake
Devils Thumb Pass
CONTINENTAL DIVIDE
TRAIL
Skyscraper Reservoir
Woodland Lake
Woodland
Bob Lake
Betty Lake
South Fork
King Lake
BM 11551
Yankee
BM 11264
Jenny Lake
Corona Lake
FOREST
Corona (Site)
Rollins Pass
BM 11671
BOULDER CO
GILPIN CO
GRAND
IDAHO

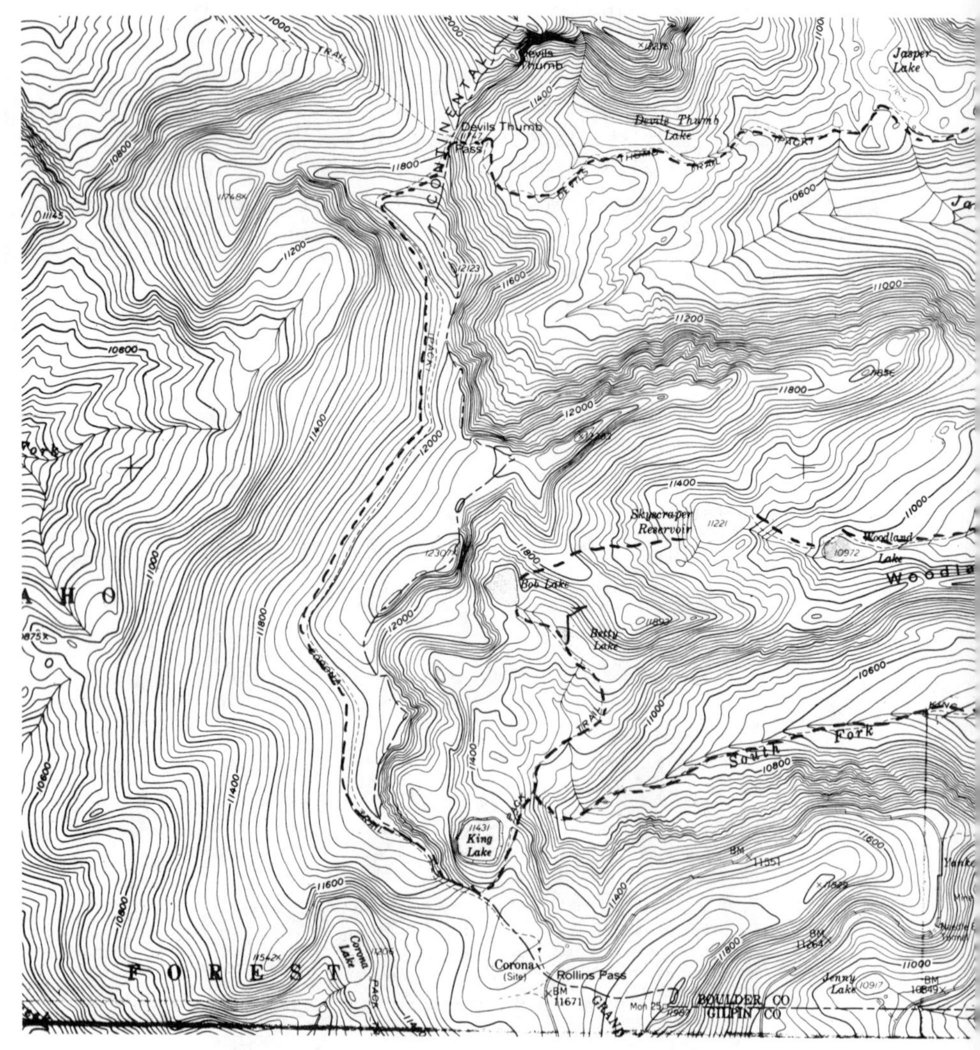

70

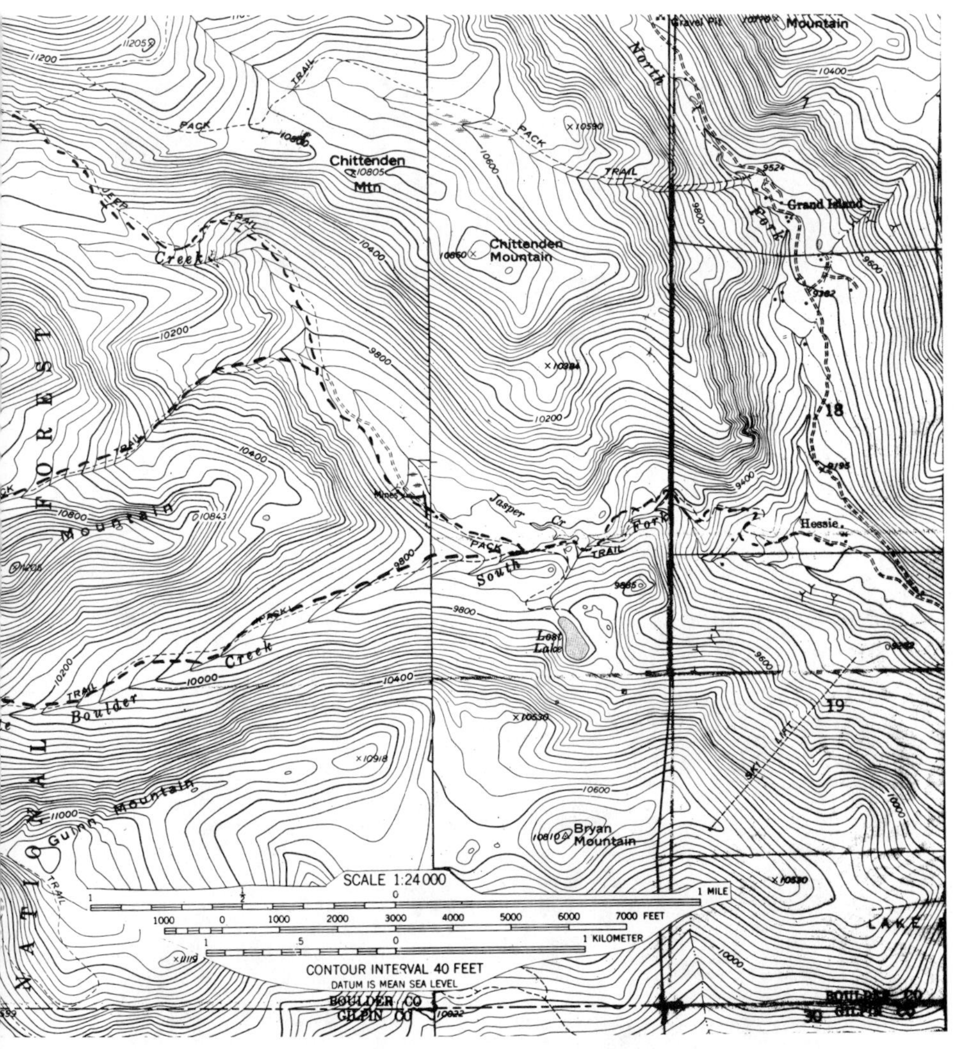

11200
11205
Chittenden
Mtn
10805
Gravel Pit
Mountain
10400
North
10590
PACK
TRAIL
9524
Grand Island
9800
Fork
Chittenden
Mountain
10650
10600
10400
9584
Creek
10200
9800
18
10984
JEEP
FOREST
10200
10400
Mountain
10843
10800
Jasper Cr
9400
Hessie
PACK
South
TRAIL
Fork
9800
9800
9888
Lost
Lake
9600
10200
Creek
10000
Boulder
10400
19
TRAIL
10918
10530
10000
10600
11000
Guinn Mountain
Bryan
10810
Mountain
11000
TRAIL
10530
SCALE 1:24 000
1
0
1 MILE
LAKE
1000   0   1000   2000   3000   4000   5000   6000   7000 FEET
1   .5   0   1 KILOMETER
10000
1119
CONTOUR INTERVAL 40 FEET
DATUM IS MEAN SEA LEVEL
BOULDER CO
GILPIN CO
10932
BOULDER CO
GILPIN CO
30

King Lake

Betty and Bob Lakes

Skyscraper Reservoir and Woodland Lake shown farther to the west

If you should decide to visit all of the lakes in the area, take this hike as described until you pass King Lake. The aerial photo should be of assistance in the rest of the traverse. Wind down from King Lake and cross the stream. After 1 mile, and just beyond this creek, there is a faint path off to the left that follows the stream bed for a short distance. Go to the right and continue climbing to the southeast end of Betty Lake.

To reach Bob Lake, go across the inlet creek from Betty Lake. Stay along the southwest shore, and then, keeping the inlet creek from Bob Lake on your right, continue climbing to the south shore of Bob Lake.

From here a topographical map is quite helpful since there is no trail to Skyscraper Reservoir. Climb east over the ridge. Once on top of the ridge, you can see Skyscraper Reservoir. Go around the southeast side of it and watch for the trail on the northeast corner of the lake. This trail will take you back to Woodland Lake. There is a good trail the remainder of the way back to the original King Lake fork and back to your car.

Total round trip distance: approximately 15 miles

Jenny Lind Gulch

Jumbo Mountain

The access to this area is through private property, so hiking through the beginning part of the area is not guaranteed.

To reach the trailhead, drive approximately 20 miles to Rollinsville from Boulder either via Highway 119 through Nederland, or take Highway 93 to its intersection with Coal Creek Canyon. Follow Coal Creek Canyon west to where it meets Highway 119 coming from Nederland, and turn south, following the road for a short distance to Rollinsville. The Rawlins Pass, or Corona Pass, Road turns west from here.

Drive on the Rawlins Pass Road for 4 miles. Here you will see a barbed-wire gate and a green and white sign posted on a tree off the road to the south which says, "No vehicles, camping or fires." The turn-out in front of this area will take only a few cars. Park here and follow the jeep road to the south.

After you reach the first fork in the road, keep to the right, since the left fork goes to private property. Continue hiking south for approximately one mile. Soon you come to a small creek which crosses the road, and another road turns right going west. Stay with the road heading south, crossing the stream. Here the road begins to climb more steeply. At the next fork, stay to the right. Continue climbing south until you are just about out of the trees. From here the road turns east for a short distance before going north.

At this point, you can see all kinds of jeep roads crisscrossing the mountain. If you stay with the road going northeast, you can climb Jumbo Mountain (9,959 feet).

Distance to Jumbo one way: approximately 4 miles
Elevation gain: 1,165 feet

Should you decide to take the road going east and climbing the hill, you will come to the next ridge on which there is an old mine and some old cabins. The road then continues to the Tip Top Mine.

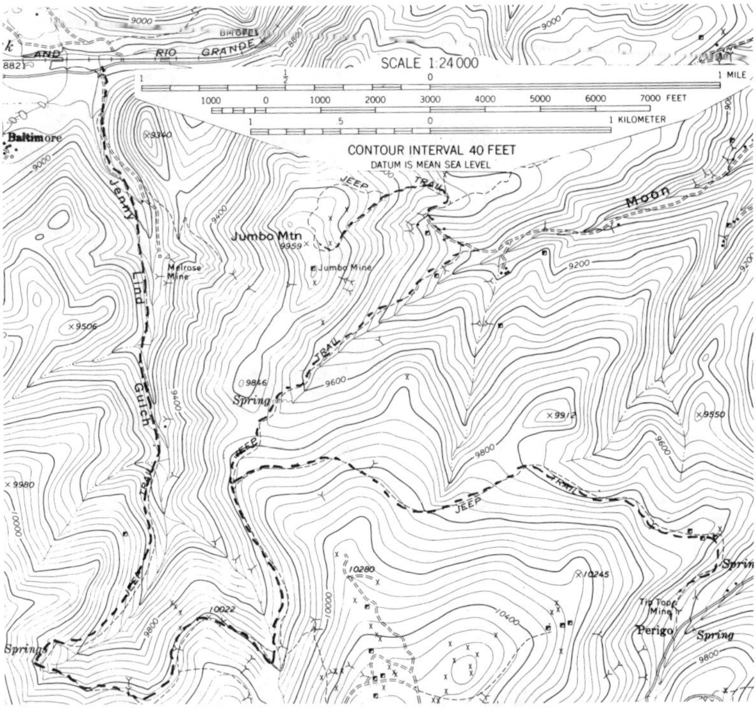

Jenny Lind Gulch trailhead

Old mining shack at Jenny Gulch

Old mining equipment found in Jenny Lind Gulch

Golden Gate Park

Black Bear

Horseshoe

Buffalo

Burro

Blue Grouse

Ground Squirrel

Mule Deer

Elk Trail

Coyote

Raccoon

Showshoe Hare

Mountain Lion

Eagle

Golden Gate Loop Hikes

Golden Gate State Park is located about one hour from Boulder via Highway 93 to the north of Golden where you turn west onto Highway 70. Another route is to leave Boulder via Highway 119 up Boulder Canyon and continue with this road through Nederland as it goes south. This road also connects with Highway 70, which takes you to Golden Gate Park.

There are many trails in the area, all of which have been marked with animal tracks. The elevation of the area ranges from 7,600 to 10,400 feet. Trail difficulty ratings have been done by the state park.

Golden Gate aerial: Kriley Pond is in the foreground with Slough Pond just below. The road circling the mountain is Mountain Base Road. Blackman Meadow is in the upper left.

This is an area that doesn't appear to be very well known. During the time the area was checked out, there were few other hikers there. The area is heavily wooded and has some good high points from which to view the surrounding terrain. It also has some old cabins in some of the meadows, which are fun to explore.

Upon entering the park, you must purchase either a daily park pass for $3.00 or an annual pass for $25.00.

The trails may be walked individually for shorter hikes, or combined with others, making longer hikes.

Southern Trailheads

A. *Black Bear Trail:* The trailhead is located at Ralston Roost, .3 mile from the Visitor's Center at the east side of the park. This is one of the most difficult trails in the park because of its steepness.

Distance: 1.9 miles one way
Elevation gain: 1,000 feet
Rating: Difficult

B. *Horseshoe Trail:* The trailhead is at Ralston Creek which is .1 mile east of the Black Bear Trail. The trail winds upward until

78

Golden Gate Park: Black Bear Trail signpost

Black bear footprint used on trail post

it comes into Frazer Meadow near some old cabins.

Distance: 2.3 miles one way
Elevation gain: 800 feet
Rating: Easy

C. Buffalo Trail: Begin at Bridge Creek or continue around the corner on the road to the Knotts Pond Trailhead. The trail

Horseshoe Trail

Horseshoe trail marker

climbs, passing a pond and more abandoned cabins, ending up at the group camp site at Rifleman Phillips Trailhead on Gap Road.

Distance: 3.2 miles one way
Elevation gain: 1,000 feet
Rating: Easy

D. Burro Trail: This one can be picked up at Bridge Creek. The trail follows a service road for a short distance before heading north. It goes to some rock quarries for those of you who are rock hounds. This trail also follows a stream for a short time, and is quite delightful.

Distance: 5.5 miles one way
Elevation gain: 400 feet
Rating: Easy

E. Blue Grouse Trail: One trailhead is at Slough Pond, .4 mile west of the Visitor's Center in the east part of the park, with the other one beginning at Kriley Pond. The trail climbs the hill to where it intersects Ground Squirrel Trail. The forest land on top is quite peaceful, since it is so deserted.

Distance: 2.3 miles one way
Elevation gain: 1,134 feet
Rating: Difficult

Blue Grouse and Ground Squirrel meet here

F. Ground Squirrel Trail: This trail begins at Kriley Pond west of the Visitor's Center and climbs to Rim Meadow.

Distance: 2 miles one way
Elevation gain: 800 feet
Rating: Moderate

Blue Grouse trail sign

Kriley Pond trailhead for Ground Squirrel Trail

Ground Squirrel sign

Close-up of Ground Squirrel footprint

Western Trailheads

A. *Mule Deer Trail:* This trail begins on Lower Mountain Base Road and continues through Rim and Frazer meadows and ends at Panorama Point.

Distance: 4.6 miles one way
Elevation gain: 1,000 feet
Rating: Easy

B. *Elk Trail:* This can be picked up on the west side of Mountain Base Road at the Mountain Base Trailhead. It passes Bootleg Bottom on the west side, and ends up at Panorama Point. To hike to the Reverend Ridge Campground, watch for Raccoon Trail which leads you back to the Visitor's Center.

Distance: 3 miles one way
Elevation gain: 1,000 feet
Rating: Easy

Elk Trail signpost

Elk footprint trail marker

C. Coyote Trail: This begins at Bootleg Bottom. It climbs through an aspen-pine forest to the top of the ridge, where the hiker gets a good overlook of the mountains to the west. The trail at the top of the ridge is definitely a "heads up" situation, since it crosses some rocks. Watch for the trail continuing off to the north. Coyote Trail ends at Frazer Meadow.

Distance: 2.2 miles one way
Elevation gain: 1,313 feet
Rating: Difficult

Coyote signpost

Raccoon trail marker

D. Raccoon Trail: This begins east of the Reverend Ridge Campground Headquarters. It goes down to the creek and then climbs back up to the east for an overlook area at Panorama Point. There you will find two good displays pointing out all of the mountains visible from this point.

> **Distance: 1.3 miles one way**
> **Elevation gain: 200 feet**
> **Rating: Moderate**

Eastern Trailhead

A. Snowshoe Hare Trail: If you begin at the Aspen Meadow Campground, you can take this trail for a short distance to Dude's Fishing Hole. If you continue southwest, you will intersect either Raccoon Trail, a short distance from Panorama Point, or Elk Trail going to the south.

> **Distance: 3.2 miles**
> **Elevation gain: approximately 400 feet**
> **Rating: Moderate**

B. Mountain Lion Trail: It begins at Nott Creek east of the Red Barn Group Picnic Area and winds around on the east side of the park to end at Forgotten Valley.

Snowshoe Hare Trail
in winter

Distance: 5.9 miles
Elevation gain: 1,100 feet
Rating: Easy

C. Eagle Trail: This also begins at Nott Creek and goes up to City Lights Ridge.

Distance: 2.1 miles
Elevation gain: 400 feet
Rating: Easy

Golden Gate Loop Hikes

A. Begin on Horseshoe Trail and follow it to its intersection with Coyote Trail in Frazer Meadow. The Coyote Trail then climbs to 9,200 feet before returning to the Bootleg Bottom picnic area. You might wish to stop for lunch there.

After lunch, cross the Mountain Base Road heading west to where Elk Trail comes in. Take this trail south down to a meadow with an old mining cabin. Watch for the trail continuing east from here, staying on the north side of the road.

Once you reach Mountain Base Road again, pick up Mule Deer Trail, and then take Ground Squirrel Trail back to Horseshoe Trail and out.

Distance: approximately 11 miles round trip
Elevation gain: approximately 3,100 feet

B. Begin at Bootleg Bottom picnic area. Pick up the Elk Trail going north to where it meets Snowshoe Hare Trail. Then intersect Mule Deer Trail near Gap Road near Lazy Squaw and follow it through Frazer Meadow to Mountain Base Road. Cross the road and pick up the southern end of Elk Trail.

Distance: approximately 8 miles round trip
Elevation gain: approximately 2,400 feet

C. Beginning at Reverend Ridge Campground on the Raccoon Trail, follow Raccoon to the bottom of the hill where it intersects Elk Trail. Take Elk Trail to Snowshoe Hare Trail. Stay with Snowshoe Hare Trail as far as Gap Road. Then hike to the right along Gap Road for a short distance until reaching Panorama Point. Return to the campground via Raccoon Trail.

Distance: approximately 5 miles round trip
Elevation gain: approximately 400 feet

Panorama Point overlooking the Continental Divide

Cabin in Black Man Meadow

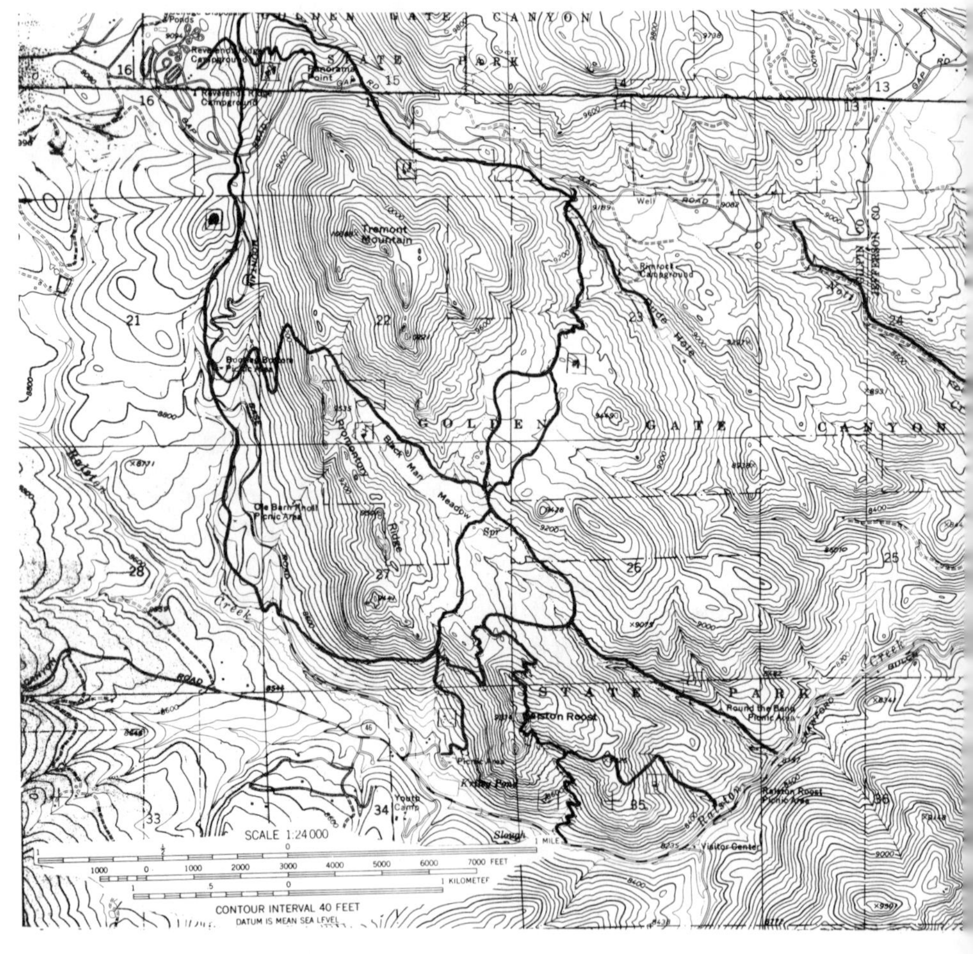
GOLDEN GATE CANYON
STATE PARK
Panorama Point
Reverends Ridge Campground
Reverends Ridge Campground
Tremont Mountain
Well ROAD
Rimrock Campground
GOLDEN GATE CANYON
Black Man Meadow
Ole Barn Knoll Picnic Area
Ralston Roost
STATE PARK
Round the Bend Picnic Area
Ralston Roost Picnic Area
Visitor Center
Youth Camp
Slough
SCALE 1:24 000
1000   0   1000   2000   3000   4000   5000   6000   7000 FEET
1   5   0   1 KILOMETER
1 MILE
CONTOUR INTERVAL 40 FEET
DATUM IS MEAN SEA LEVEL

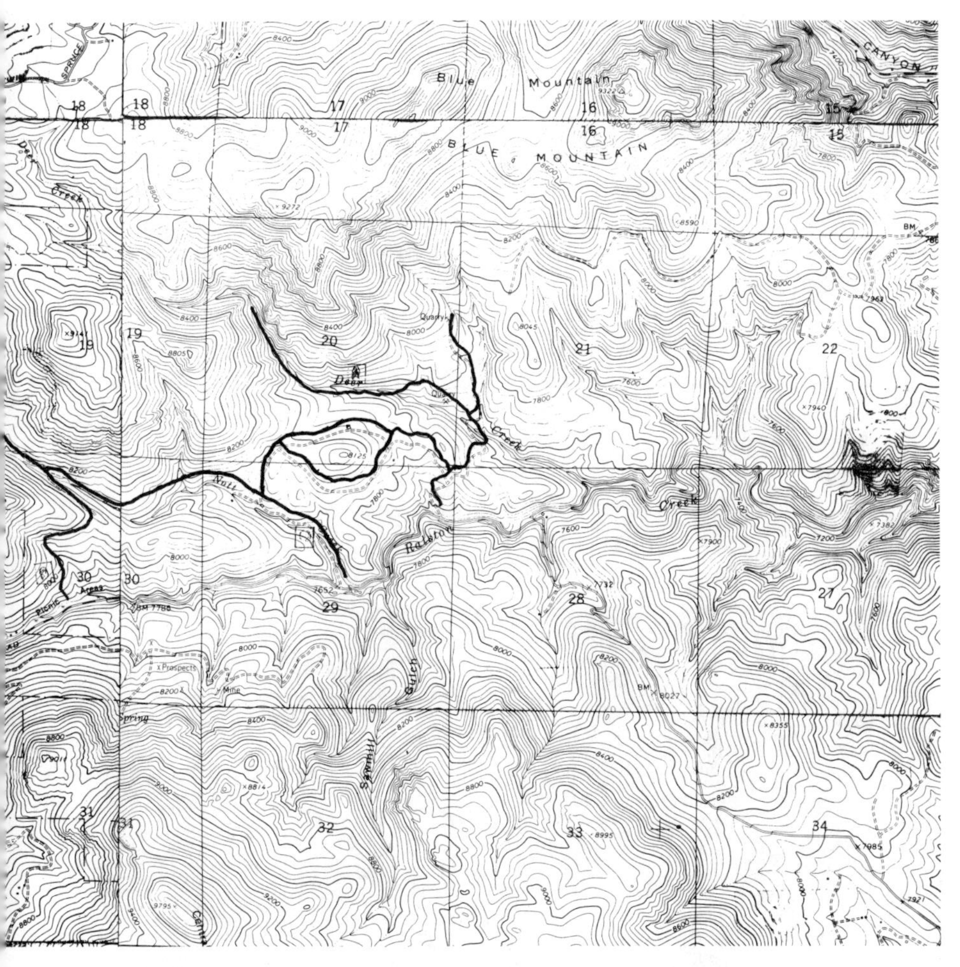

CANYON
Blue Mountain
9322
BLUE MOUNTAIN
Deer
Creek
18 18 17 16 15
18 18 17 16 15
9272
8590
BM
19 20 21 22
Quarry
9341
Deep
7600
7940
8125
Null
Creek
Ralston
Creek
7382
30 30 29 28 21
Picnic
Area
BM 7788
7732
Prospect
Mine
Spring
BM 8027
8355
Sawmill
Gulch
31 31 32 33 34
8814
8995
7985
9795
Canyon

Left Hand Canyon Trails

Public Access

Nugget Hill

The Boulder foothills are full of old mining roads that criss-cross in many places, offering some very scenic hiking. Since many of these roads are quite steep, hiking boots can make a safer hike.

Public Access Road–Left Hand Canyon: This is a steep, old mining road that takes the hiker up to a good rock overlook of the plains to the east. It passes by several old mines along the way.

To reach the jeep road, take Highway 36 toward Lyons. Turn west by the Greenbriar Restaurant onto Highway 61. Continue 2.6 miles to the Buckingham picnic area. Turn right again. The Public Access Road is about 1 mile from Buckingham Park on the north side of the road.

Since this road is also used frequently by motorcyclists, it has many side trails going off in different directions, making it neces-

Public Access Road. The road bypasses several mines before curving back to climb to the rocky overlook at the top of the mountain.

sary for the hiker to keep track of landmarks in order to return to the car.

Once on top, the hiker has a good selection of rocks to scramble on, and from which to enjoy a tremendous view while eating lunch. If you continue to follow the road along the top, you will reach private property.

Distance: 7.5 miles round trip
Elevation gain: approximately 700 feet

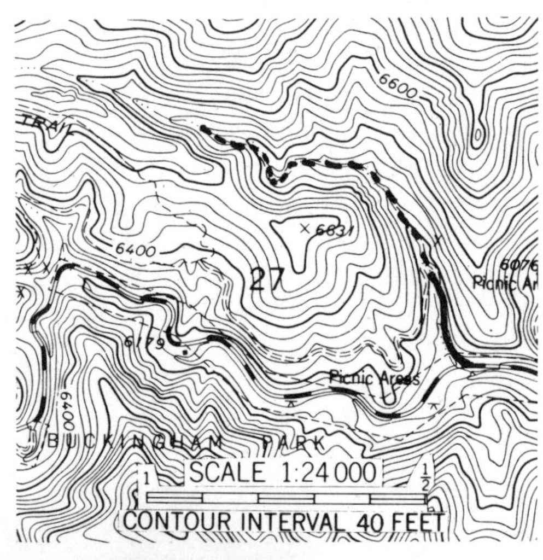

Road winds through
a beautiful forest

Nugget Hill: This is another steep, yet picturesque mining road. To reach its beginning, located 14 miles from Boulder's northern city limits, take Highway 36 toward Lyons. Upon reaching the Greenbriar Restaurant, turn west onto Highway 61. Continue for 2.6 miles to the Buckingham picnic area. Now turn right. After 2.8 miles, you will come to another intersection. Take the left turn for Ward (Highway 106). After 3.8 miles, you will come to the old dirt mining road which is located just outside the town of Rowena. This town is not marked in any way, but has several houses clustered there.

After you have crossed the bridge just outside the town, watch for four mailboxes off to your right. They are just below an old large black box placed by the miners along the side of the road.

This road takes the hiker by several old mines. At the first major intersection, take the road going to the left. The right-hand fork will take you to another old mine. Then upon reaching the shoulder, the road again forks. Take the right-hand road going uphill and to the east. This road crosses one ridge and then drops down for a short distance before climbing to the top of Nugget Hill.

Nugget trailhead: Crucial that the hiker find this black miner's box to be sure of being on the right road.

This is a good fall hike because there are many aspen trees along the ridge. It might be a good one to avoid in the late spring during tick season.

Distance: 5 miles round trip
Elevation gain: 1,362 feet

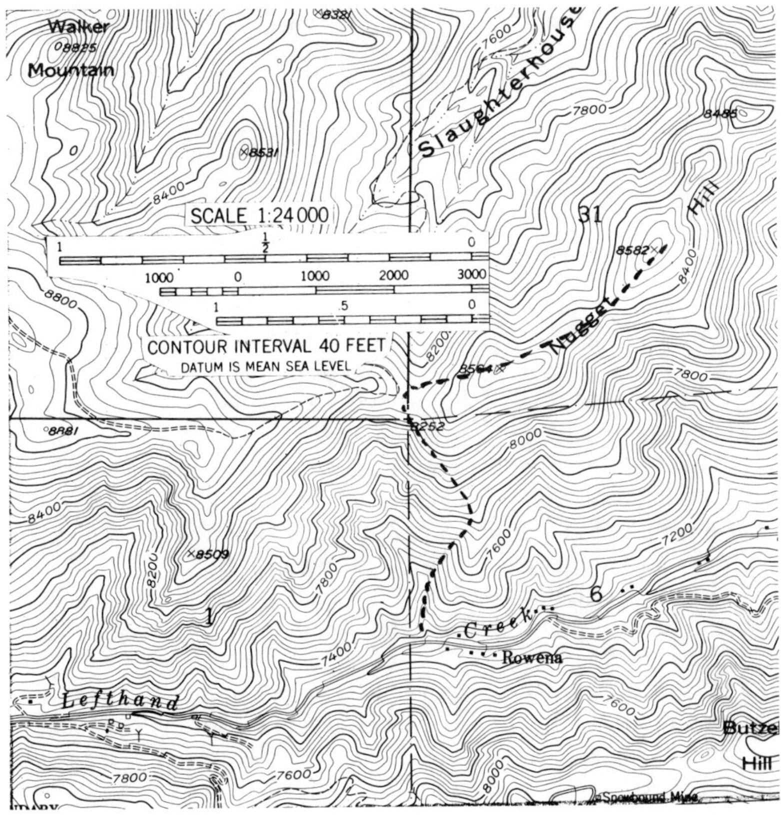

Switzerland Trail of America and Sugarloaf Mountain

Switzerland Trail of America: This is an old track bed of a railroad route built by the Colorado and Northwestern Railroad in 1898. Starting in Boulder, its route ran westerly to the intersection of Boulder and Four Mile creeks. From here, it ran northwest, passing Crisman, Salina, Wall Street, Copper Rock, and then into Sunset.

At Sunset, the line divides, with one branch going to Eldora and the other to Ward. On the latter route, the train passed by or close to most of the most valuable mining claims of Boulder County.

Since this is an old railroad bed, the grade is quite gradual, making hiking quite enjoyable.

Accesses to this trail include the following:

1. Go up Boulder Canyon 5 miles to the Sugarloaf turn-off. Follow Sugarloaf Road uphill until you reach its top and the pavement ends. This is another 4.2 miles. At this point you will see 6 mailboxes off on the north side of the road where another dirt road meets the Sugarloaf Road. Follow this road to the north, keeping to the right at the first fork, and continuing on to the west. After .8 mile, you will come to the Switzerland Trail.

If you park here, you can either hike to the left on the Eldora branch to reach Glacier Lake in 5.5 miles, or hike to your right to Sunset in 4 miles.

2. Go to Gold Hill via Sunshine Canyon. Upon reaching town, continue to the west for an additional 3 miles to another section of the Switzerland Trail. Here the trail may be taken to the south for 1 mile to the Mount Alto picnic area, and an additional 3 miles to Sunset.

If you follow the Switzerland Trail to the north, you will have a fairly level 3.5-mile hike around the side of the mountain. Toward the end of the hike, the road narrows, becoming a footpath that goes over a rockfall below the main road leading to Lefthand Canyon.

3. Go up Boulder Canyon to the Four Mile Canyon turn-off (2.4 miles). Drive 11 miles up Four Mile Canyon to Sunset. From here, you can hike 4 miles to Glacier Lake or 4 miles to Sugarloaf.

4. Glacier Lake Access: Take Highway 119 from Nederland,

Sugarloaf Mountain. Sugarloaf is in the foreground. The Switzerland Trail circles Sugarloaf with the left side of the road going to Glacier Lake and the right branch going to Sunset.

heading north. When you reach the Sugarloaf turn-off, you are 2.5 miles from the Glacier Lake Road. The turn-off is marked by a Forest Service access sign on the east side of the highway.

The Glacier Lake area is one that was highly popular when the old narrow gauge railroad came from Boulder to the lodge at the lake. Unfortunately, the lodge has since been gutted by fire, but the old stone walls and old fireplace in the courtyard remain.

If you hike from Glacier Lake to Sunset, the distance is 9.5 miles. This hike might be a good one for a car key exchange.

Sugarloaf Mountain: To reach this mountain, take Boulder Canyon west for 5 miles to the Sugarloaf turn-off. Follow the Sugarloaf Road up to the top of the hill where the pavement ends after about 4 miles. There you will find 6 mailboxes beside a dirt road going to the north. Follow this road, keeping to the right at the one fork, and then continuing west for .8 mile. Park here near the Switzerland Trail and look for an unmarked mining road going uphill to the northeast. This road leads to a fantastic overlook of the mountains to the west and the valley to the east. The Arapaho Indians used this lookout as a signaling point.

Distance: 1 mile one way
Elevation gain: 476 feet

Glacier Lake. Highway 119 is at the bottom, and the
Switzerland Trail is on the right.

Glacier Lake

Old lodge at Glacier Lake where the Switzerland Trail ride once dropped picnickers. Now located on private property.

Gulch
Tuscarora
FOREST
Larkhead
Gulch
Creek
8600
8400
8200
8600
8400
9000
9200
9000
8800
8800
8600
8
7
12
9314
9432
9401
8833
9721
9000
8800
9000
18
18
17
13
9274
BM
160
8883
8561
9441
9161
8754
Routt Gulch
8338
BM
9074
9079
Sunset
8600
14
9000
19
19
Fourmile
20
8200
8000
Creek
8591
8256
9200
8800
8800
8600
8400
Pennsylvania
8909
Gulch
8366
Bear
8600
9000
8800
8925
BM 9112
9200
Glacier
Lake
Glacier
Lake
25
30
30
29
8723
9065
SCALE 1:24 000
9017
8800
CONTOUR INTERVAL 40 FE
DATUM IS MEAN SEA LEVEL

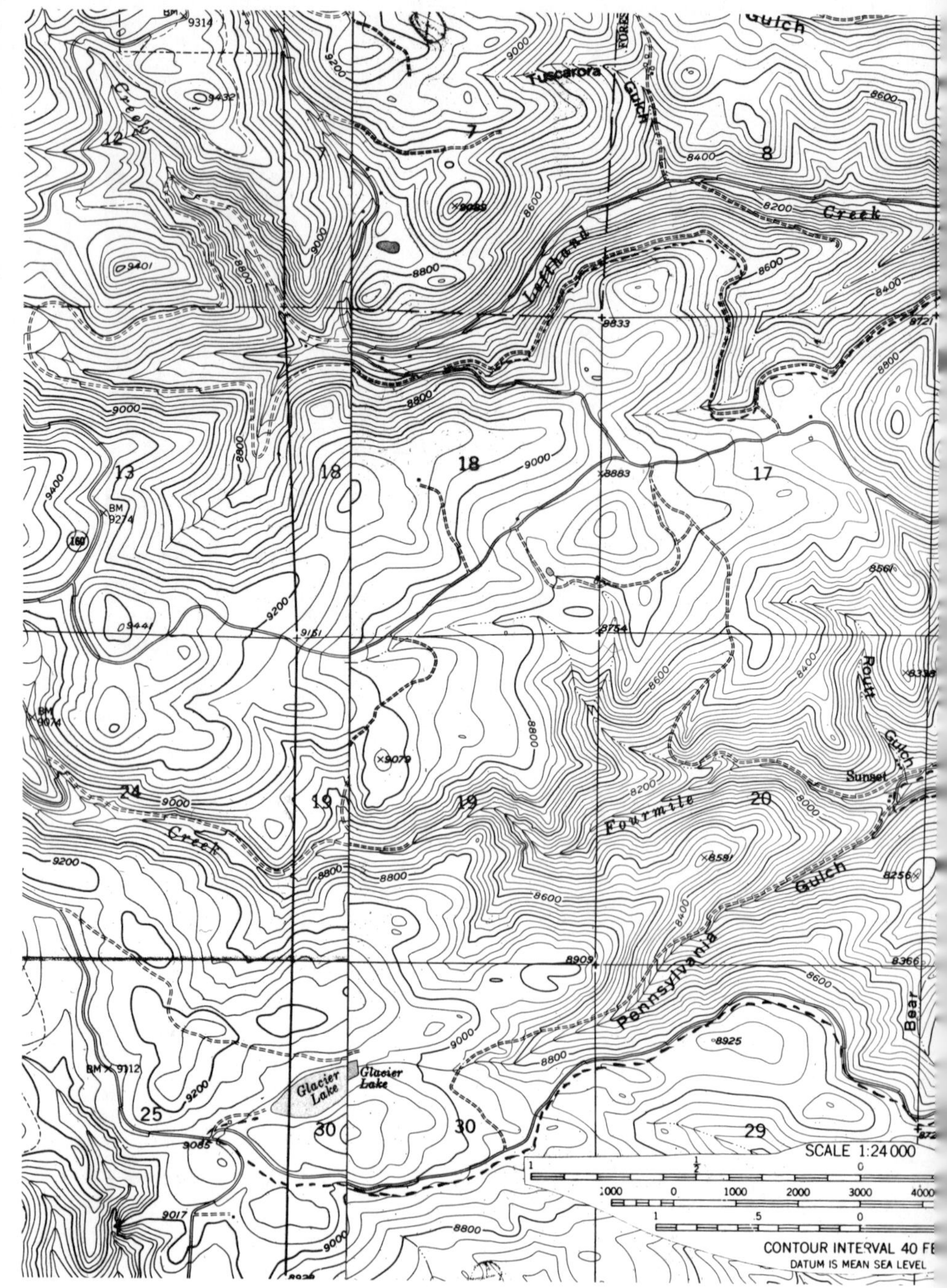

100

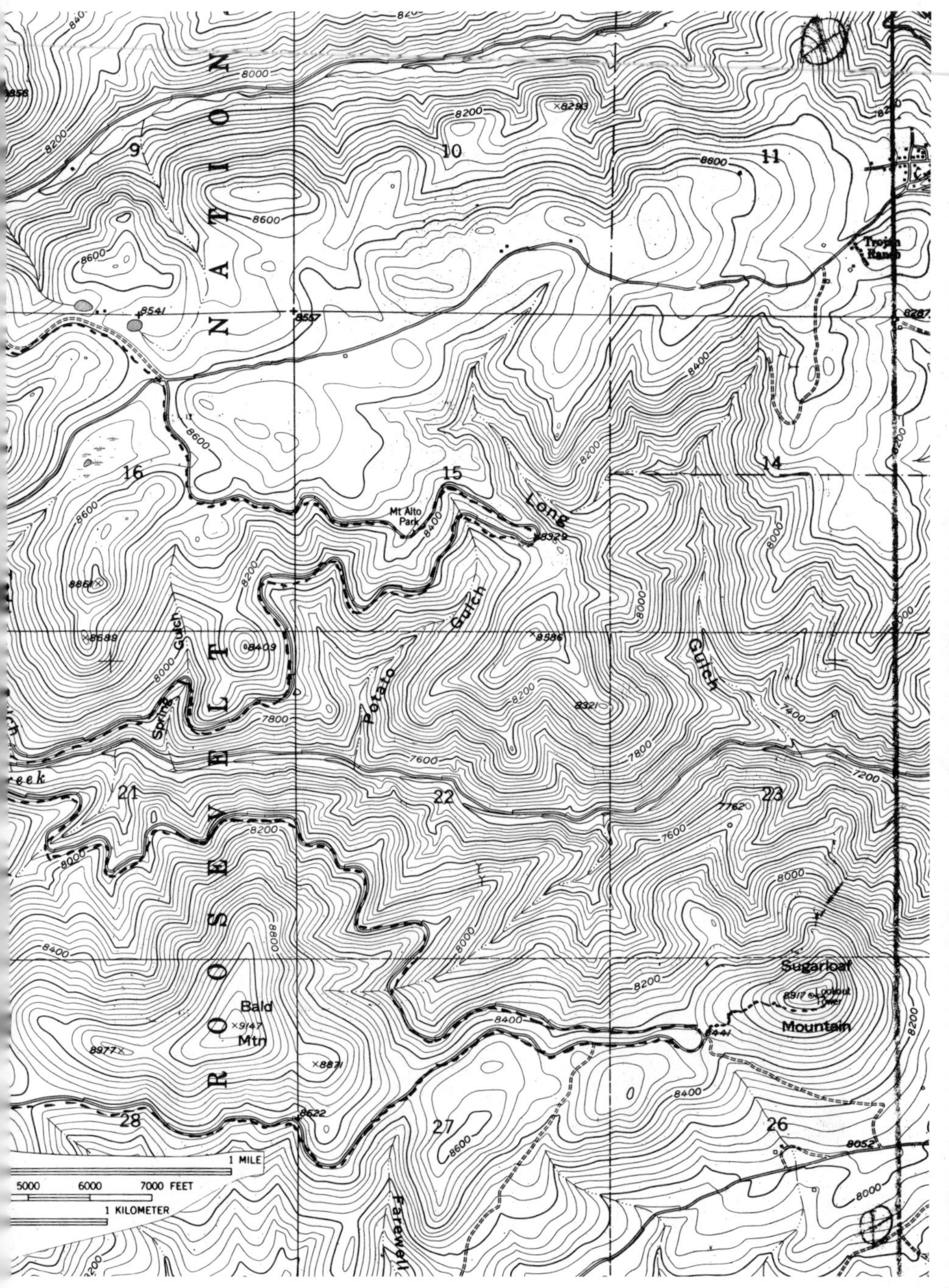
NATIONAL
ROOSEVELT
9
10
11
Trojan Ranch
16
15
14
Long
Mt Alto Park
Potato Gulch
Gulch
Spring Gulch
Creek
21
22
23
Bald Mtn
Sugarloaf
Lookout Tower
Mountain
28
27
26
Farewell
1 MILE
5000   6000   7000 FEET
1 KILOMETER

Thorodin Mountain

To reach the trailhead, take Highway 93 out of Boulder to Highway 72, Coal Creek Canyon. Follow Coal Creek to the west. Upon reaching the Coal Creek Canyon Inn, you are 2 miles west of the turn-off for Thorodin. The trailhead is 19 miles from Boulder.

Turn south on Camp Eden Road and follow this road until it dead-ends at the Axton Ranch. Since this is private property, permission should be obtained from the owner of the ranch at 642-3414.

The trail climbs through a forest, bypassing some good raspberry-picking bushes. Once on top, you reach the fire lookout as well as a picnic table where you can have your lunch. The hike offers some good views of the plains and mountains, and gives a good idea as to why a fire lookout was placed on its top.

Distance: 6 miles round trip
Elevation gain: 1,500 feet

The Axton Ranch: Thorodin Mountain trailhead

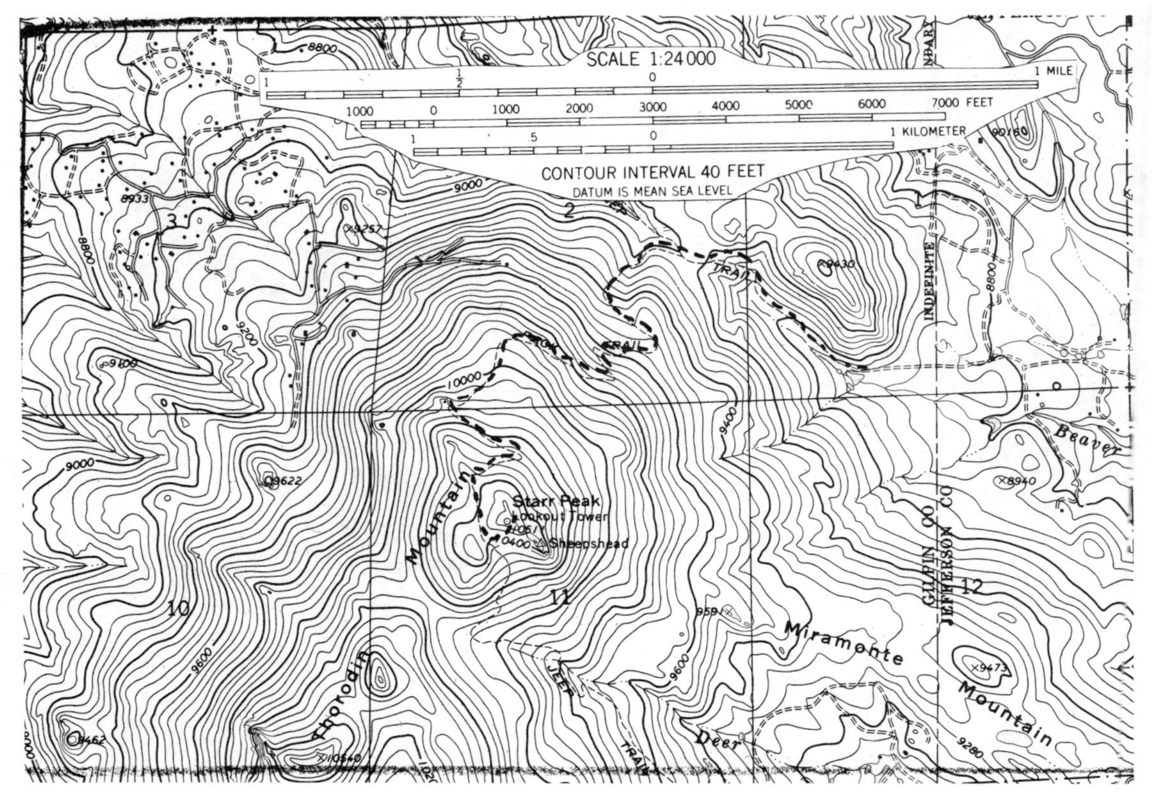

SCALE 1:24000
1 MILE
1 KILOMETER
7000 FEET
1000   0   1000   2000   3000   4000   5000   6000
CONTOUR INTERVAL 40 FEET
DATUM IS MEAN SEA LEVEL
Beaver
Miramonte
Mountain
Deer
Thorodin
Mountain
Starr Peak
Lookout Tower
Sheepshead
GILPIN CO
JEFFERSON CO
INDEFINITE
TRAIL
JEEP
NDARY

Trail marker for Thorodin

Road portion of the trail

Walker Ranch

Meyers Homestead Trail

So. Boulder Creek

Crescent Meadows

Scenic Loop

Columbine Trail

Eldorado Canyon

The Walker Ranch is operated by Boulder County Parks and Open Space. The land was originally homesteaded by James Walker in 1873; the present ranch house was built in 1898.

To reach the ranch, take Baseline Road west to Flagstaff Road. When the Flagstaff Road turns east to go to the summit of the moun-

Walker Ranch parking area. The road inside the fence leads down to Boulder Creek.

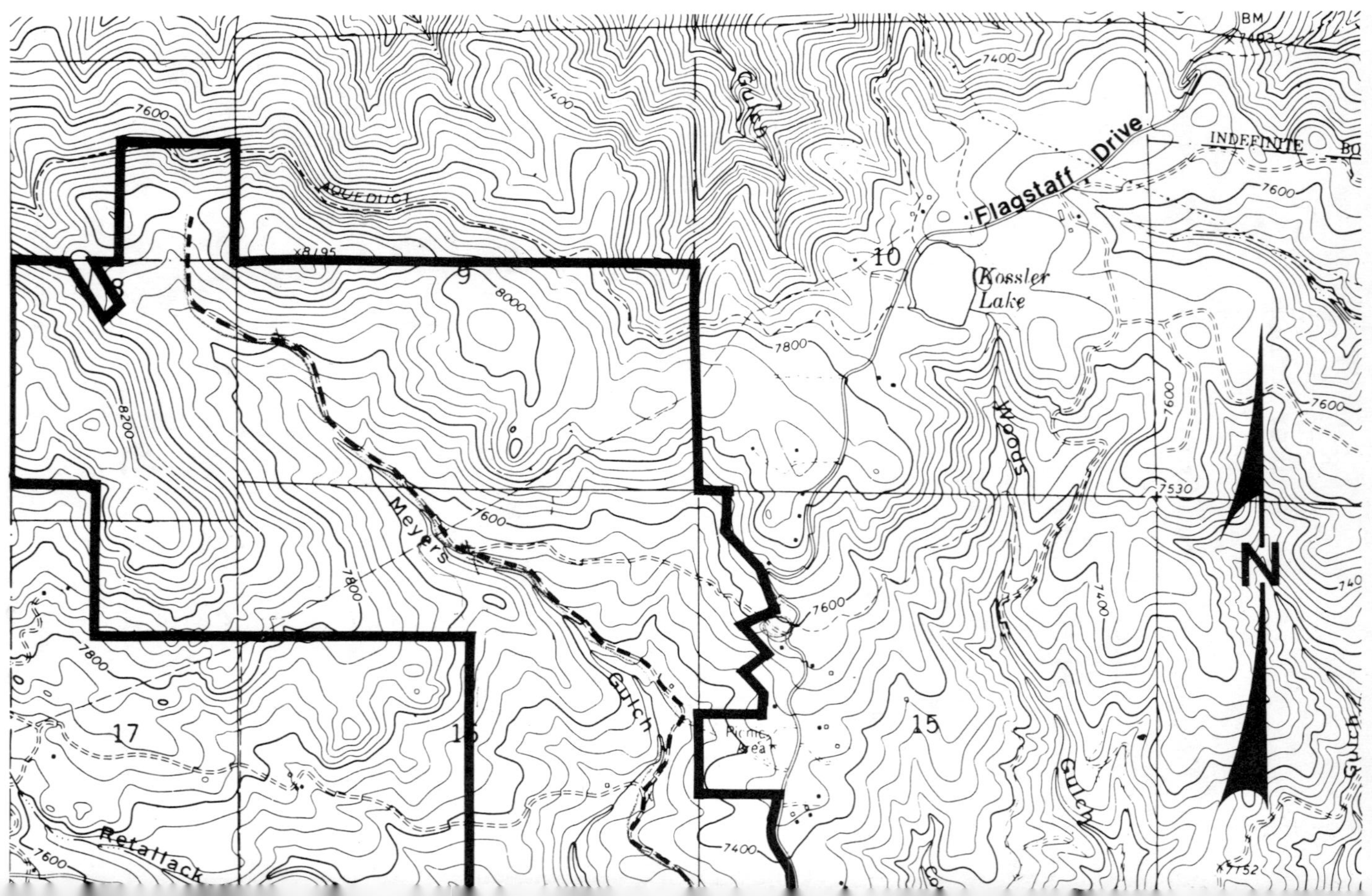

N
Flagstaff Drive
INDEFINITE BD
Kossler Lake
Woods
Gulch
AQUEDUCT
Meyers
Gulch
Ratattack
Picnic Area
BM
7400
7600
7600
7530
7600
7600
7400
7800
8000
8200
7600
7800
7800
7600
7400
7600
7752
x 8195
10
9
15
17
13

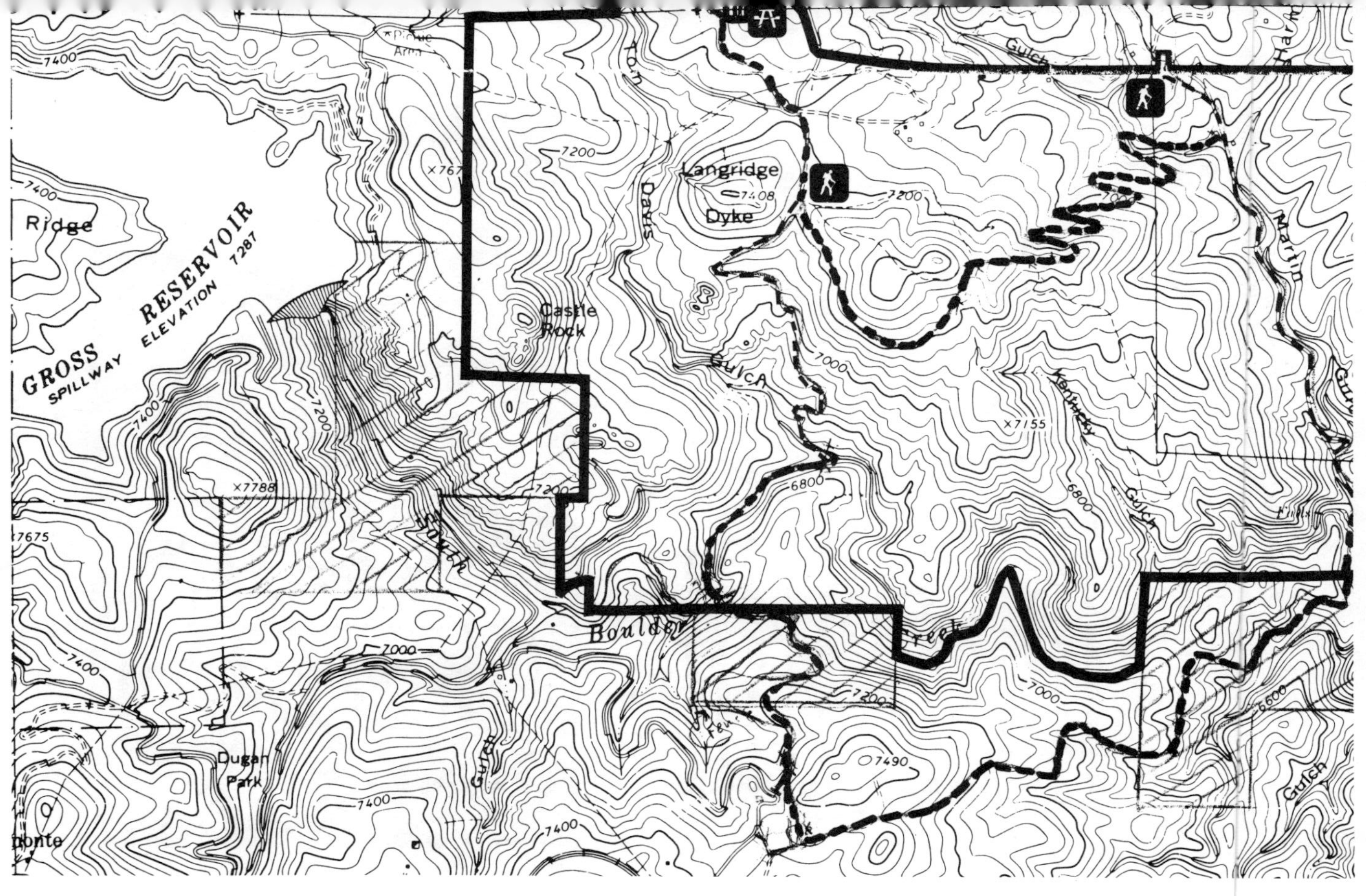

Picnic Arm
7400
7200
Langridge
7408
Dyke
7200
Ridge
7400
GROSS RESERVOIR
SPILLWAY   ELEVATION 7287
Davis
Gulch
Castle Rock
7000
7000
Gulch
×7767
×7788
7200
7200
6800
×7155
Kentucky
Gulch
6800
×7675
South
Boulder
Creek
7200
7000
7000
7490
Dugan Park
Gulch
7400
7400
7400
6800
Monte
Martin
Gulch

tain, stay with the Kossler Lake Road going west, passing Kossler Lake. The acreage is just beyond Pine Needle Notch, 7.4 miles from Baseline Road. Be alert if you hike here during hunting season, since the area is open to hunters during the rifle hunting season.

Meyers Homestead Trail: The trail begins from the parking lot next to the picnic pavilion on the right side of the road by Walker Ranch. At first the trail crosses through some open meadows. Then, after a half mile, you'll begin climbing to the crest of a ridge for a good overlook of Boulder Canyon.

Distance: 5 miles
Difficulty: Easy

For a side trip, after you've hiked a half mile, watch for a trail going west. This half-mile trail passes an historic mill site.

Distance: 2.5 miles to trail's end
Elevation gain: 600 feet
Difficulty: Moderate

Boulder Creek: scene of good fly-fishing

Meadow at end of Meyers Gulch

South Boulder Creek Trail: Park in the lot on the east side of Flagstaff Road and south of the Walker Ranch buildings. One short hike from here is down to Boulder Creek, where you can enjoy some fly-fishing for trout or enjoy a picnic at one of the tables beside the creek.

Distance: 1 mile one way
Elevation gain: 560 feet
Difficulty: Moderate

Crescent Meadows: If you continue hiking west along the river on the South Boulder Creek Trail, you'll come to a bridge. Cross this bridge, and watch for the trail going left up the hillside. This trail, Crescent Meadows, goes to another parking area on the Gross Reservoir Road. The trail you see continuing west up Boulder Creek will dead-end after a short distance and join private property owned by the Denver Water Board.

Distance from your car to the parking lot by Crescent
** Meadows Trail: 1.5 miles**
Elevation gain: 400 feet
Difficulty: Moderate

Loop Hike: Hike down to the river on South Boulder Creek Trail. Cross the bridge and hike uphill to the southwest until you intersect an old road which takes you to the Crescent Meadows parking lot. Once you leave the lot, hike back downhill on the Crescent Meadows Trail to the river, where you'll meet the South Boulder Creek Trail. Watch for the old road which will lead you back uphill for another mile along Harmon Martin Gulch to the Eldorado Canyon Trail. To return to your car, either follow the Columbine Trail back uphill, or hike back along Bison Road and then Pika Road.

Distance for the loop: 8 miles

Columbine Trail: This trail begins from the parking lot above the Walker Ranch. Hike southeast along the trail, which swings around on the sunny side of the mountain to a great overlook of the valley to the south of you. This is a good picnic stop where you can watch the trains passing by on the opposite hillside. This trail then drops steeply down to intersect the road section of the Eldorado Canyon Trail.

Distance to here: 2.5 miles
Elevation loss: 400 feet
Difficulty: Moderately easy

To complete the loop, we hiked back along Bison Road to Pika Road and back to our car. If you prefer not to hike along the road, retrace your original route.

Distance for loop: 3.5 miles

Eldorado Canyon Trail: This trailhead is at Walker Ranch. Turn east on Pika Road and then south on Bison to reach the parking lot.

The trail begins to the east on an old road which drops downhill. However, it then begins to climb up to a wonderful overlook of the Continental Divide before dropping down into Eldorado Springs State Park.

Distance: 5.5 miles
Elevation loss: 920 feet
Difficulty: Strenuous

White Ranch

Rawhide

Wranglers Run

Waterhole

Belcher Hill

Mustang

Sawmill

Maverick

Longhorn

Jefferson County Open Space includes a very scenic park just 25.2 miles from Boulder. The area was originally homesteaded by the White family in the 1900s and served as a cattle ranch from 1903–1969.

The trails in the area go in various loops, making it possible for the hiker to take as long or as short a hike as time and desire permit without having to retrace any footsteps.

To reach White Ranch, drive toward Golden on Highway 93 to its intersection with Highway 56 (15.6 miles from Table Mesa Drive). Turn west onto the Golden Gate highway and continue to Crawford Gulch (3.9 miles farther). Turn right onto Crawford Gulch and continue for 4 more miles. Turn right again and proceed 1.4 miles to the entrance to White Ranch. The main parking area, complete with picnic tables and rest facilities, is 1.5 miles from the gate.

From the parking area, the hiker has many possibilities. All of the trails are over varying terrain with some very steep exposures. The elevation difference on the western side of the ranch is approximately 650 feet. The trails here are through beautifully wooded areas where a large herd of deer may be seen roaming.

After exploring the western loops, the hiker may wish to return to the picnic area for lunch before looking over the eastern trails.

To pick up the Belcher Hill Trail, hike west along the entrance road for .3 mile. It begins on the south side of the road. From here, descend through the woods to some small creeks. To get an overview of the entire ranch, continue with the Mustang Trail and return to the parking lot via Longhorn Trail (6.4 miles). The maximum elevation loss on this side is approximately 1,480 feet.

Should the hiker wish to make a little shorter loop but still have a good view of this extremely scenic area, the loop from Belcher Hill to Mustang Trail down to where it joins Belcher Hill and then

Trails on the White Ranch

back to Maverick and to Longhorn offers another good hike of 5.1 miles.

The trails in the eastern section have many good open viewing points where the hiker can see Ralston Reservoir out to the north as well as the various mesas out to the east.

Jefferson County has located many of these trails on the perimeter of the ranch so that the hiker can better view the wildlife in a natural setting without disturbing them. Since the diamondback rattlesnake may also be found in the park, caution should be employed around rock and rubble piles where the snakes may be found during the warmer months of the year.

Because the trails cover much steep terrain, drinking water should be carried.

White Ranch Trails
1. Rawhide 4.2 miles
2. Wranglers Run .8 mile
3. Waterhole .6 mile
4. Belcher Hill 2.5 miles
5. Mustang 2.3 miles
6. Sawmill .6 mile
7. Maverick .9 mile
8. Longhorn 2.7 miles
Outer loop of the property: 10 miles

Old log near cattle pens on the ranch

Upper Forest Lake Via
Jenny Creek and Rollins Pass

Because of the difficulty of accessing this area through private property from East Portal, you can reach the upper Forest Lake from the Lake Eldora ski area via the Jenny Creek Trail.

Park in the lower parking lot of the Lake Eldora ski area by the ski touring ticket office. Climb the hill beside the Ho Hum chairlift. Once on the top of the ski hill, turn right and follow the Foxtail ski trail as far as Upper Bunnyfair ski trail, located just below the large hill west of you.

Watch for the forest access signs and follow their trail through the woods, over a ridge, dropping down into Jenny Creek. Turn right onto the Jenny Creek jeep road and follow it toward the west, keeping Jenny Creek on your left.

After approximately 3 miles you'll have to cross a tributary creek. Continue to the left when the road forks right to climb up to the Guinn Mountain Hut.

Follow the jeep road in a westerly direction. As you near Rollins Pass, the jeep road turns to the north and climbs above timberline to join Rollins Pass.

Once you've intersected the Rollins Pass road, you may wish to take a few minutes' side trip to the northwest side of the road

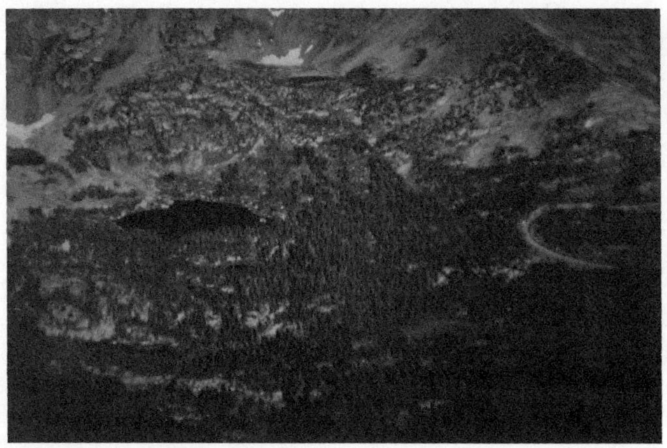

Jenny Lake seen from the top of the 6.5-mile trail

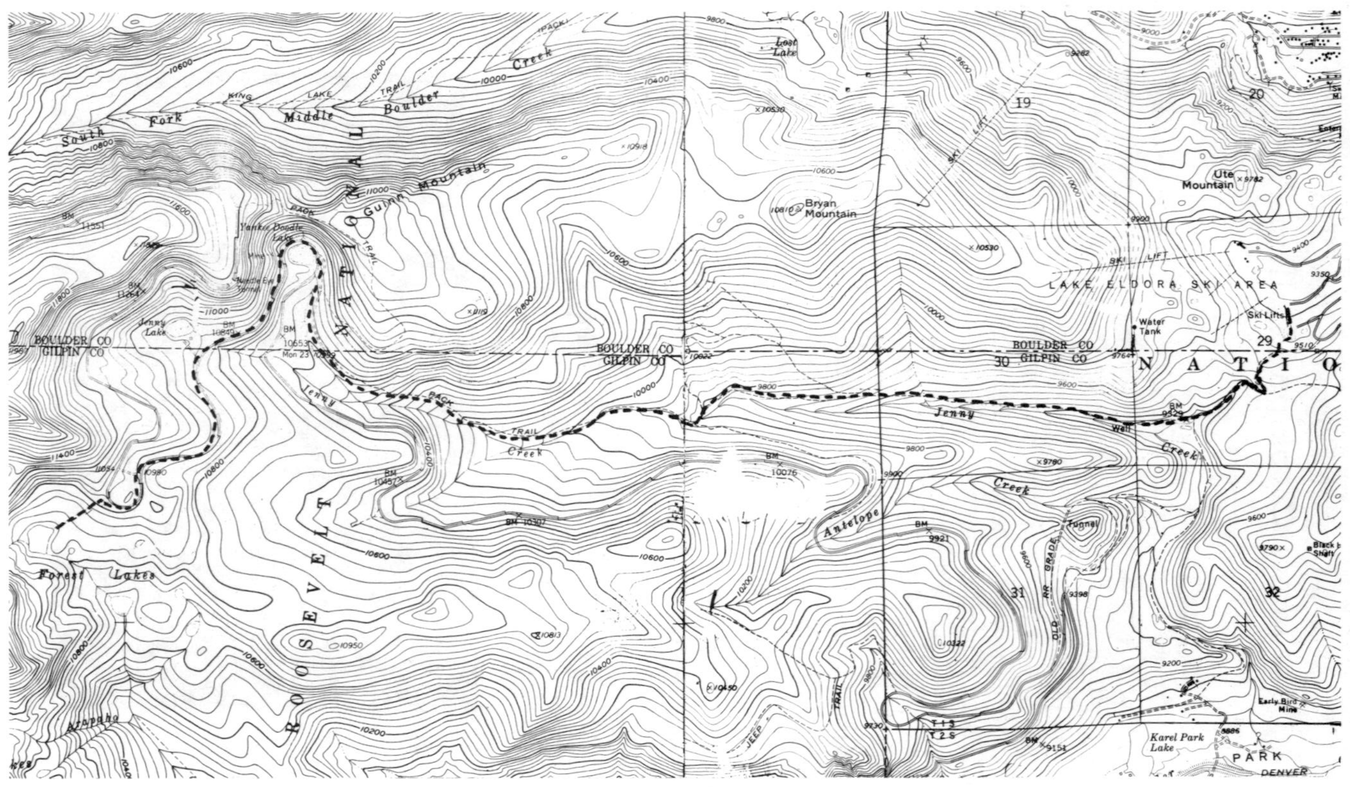
South Fork
King Lake Trail
Middle Boulder Creek
Gunn Mountain
Lost Lake
19
20
Ute Mountain
Bryan Mountain
Pack Trail
BM 11551
Yankee Doodle Lake
Guinea Ext. Tunnel
BM 11264
Jenny Lake
BM 10849
BM 10653
Mon 23
BOULDER CO / GILPIN CO
BOULDER CO / GILPIN CO
BOULDER CO / GILPIN CO
30
29
ROOSEVELT
NATIONAL
Jenny Creek
Pack Trail
BM 10457
BM 10507
BM 10076
Antelope
BM 9921
Jenny Creek
Wall Creek
Tunnel
Water Tank
Ski Lift
LAKE ELDORA SKI AREA
Ski Lift
OLD RR GRADE
31
32
Forest Lakes
BM 10813
10950
T 1 S / T 2 S
Jeep Trail
BM 9151
Black Shaft
Early Bird Mine
Karel Park Lake
Arapaho
PARK
DENVER

to take a look at Yankee Doodle Lake before proceeding on your way.

Turn left on the Rollins Pass Road and follow it past Jenny Lake, also on your right, to a hairpin turn in the road. Watch for a sign here on the right side of the road for Forest Lake. From here, there is no established trail for the last half mile down to the Upper Forest Lake. However, if you study the map and the picture, and look down to the southeast, you can soon see your destination.

Distance to lake: approximately 6.5 miles
Elevation gain: 1,727 feet
Elevation loss to the lake: approximately 200 feet

Shoshoni and Pawnee Peaks

Access to these peaks is from Indian Peaks. Drive in to Brainard Lake, off Highway 72, and take the fork to the Long Lake Trailhead.

Hike up the Pawnee Pass Trail to the pass. From here, you have the option of either hiking to the north up Pawnee Peak, bushwhacking your way to the top for 2,598 feet, or hiking to the south to climb up Shoshoni Peak.

Shoshoni doesn't have an established trail either, but since both peaks are above timberline, your route is easily picked. To climb Shoshoni from the pass entails hiking over some fields of talus up to the ridge below the peak. Once you're over the talus,

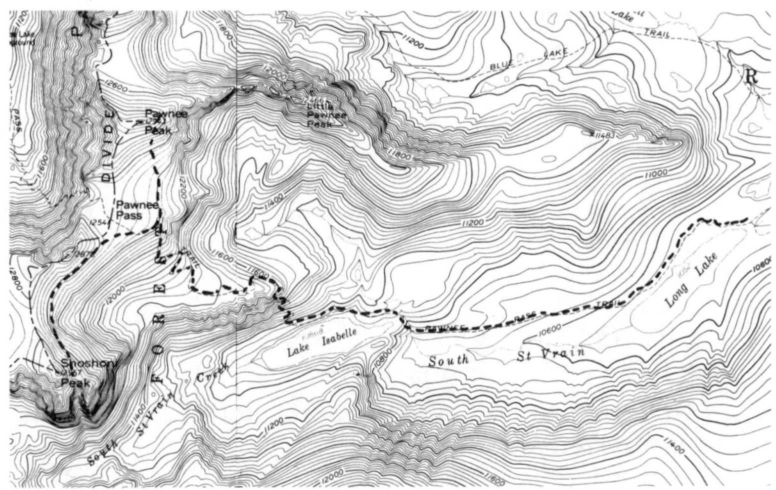

the hike to the summit is along a grassy slope. The rocks on the summit only permit a small number of climbers to be there at one time.

To return from Shoshoni, you can drop down the grassy slopes and "skate" down some scree to the grassy meadows south of the Pawnee Pass Trail.

> **Distance up Pawnee Pass: 3.7 miles**
> **Additional distance up Shoshoni: approximately 1 mile**
> **Additional distance up Pawnee Peak: approximately**
>   **.5 mile**
> **Elevation gain up Shoshoni: 2,622 feet**
> **Elevation gain up Pawnee Peak: 2,598 feet**

Arapaho Pass "Knob"

For a truly beautiful lookout over the western valleys beyond Arapaho Pass, try this hike.

It begins from the 4th of July Campground reached by driving through the town of Eldora. When the road forks on the west side of town, turn right and drive up the rough dirt road to the recently constructed parking lot at the end of the road. Now you can also enjoy a newly built trail access to Arapaho Pass, replacing the one up the jeep road.

This trail crosses several streams and comes to some of the most breathtaking wildflower displays imaginable, as you wind your way up the switchbacks to the top of the pass. This hike is particularly colorful during July and August.

Once you come to timberline, you pass a trail forking off to your right, which goes up to an overlook of Arapaho Glacier and on to Arapaho Peak. Stay to the left here and continue to the top of the pass, passing Dorothy Lake on your left.

Once on the top of the ridge, continue to follow the pass to the west, dropping down a few hundred feet to a grassy knob off to your right. Turn to the north and follow this ridge north, crossing over some rocky outcrops until reaching the last one. This is a great place to enjoy both your picnic lunch as well as a tremendous overlook of Wheeler Basin at your feet. You can also get a good view of both North and South Arapaho Peaks as well.

> **Distance: 2.8 miles to top of pass; additional 1 mile to**
>   **knob overlook**
> **Elevation gain: 1,676 feet**

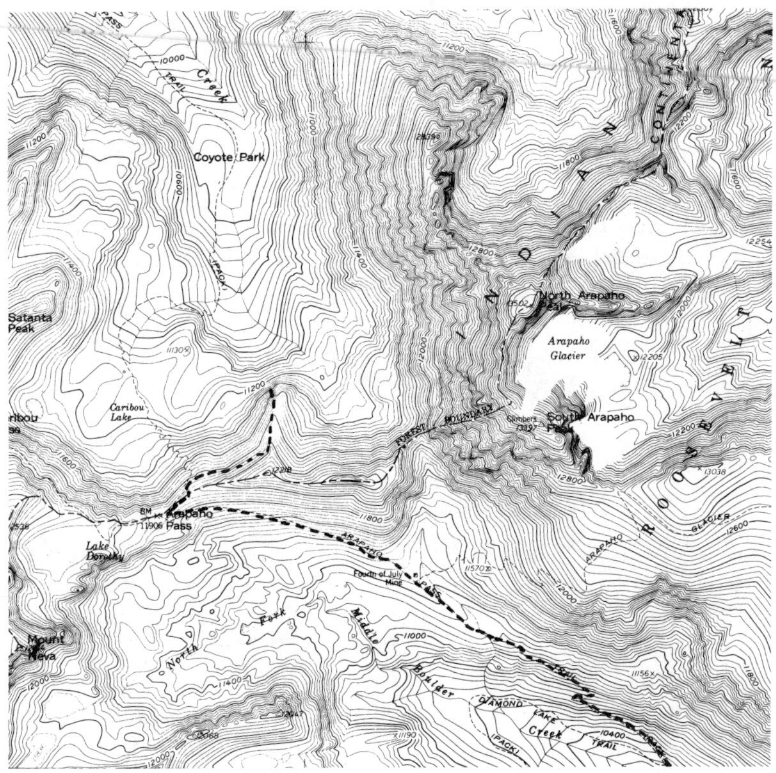

Caribou

To reach this old mining town, drive to Nederland via Boulder Canyon. Once in town, turn to the west onto Highway 72, the Peak-to-Peak Highway, and continue for .3 mile to a marked turn to the west for Caribou.

This dirt road climbs for 5 miles up to 10,003 feet to the old town of Caribou. Not much is left of this town today except the old stone smelter.

Caribou was the site of a rich silver lode in 1869, and within a year of its discovery the area was overrun with mines. Within a short time, over 3,000 inhabitants had moved in. At first they lived in tents, but gradually built wooden buildings.

The community boasted five saloons, and two hotels: Planter's House and Sherman House, which were known from coast to coast for their fine meals.

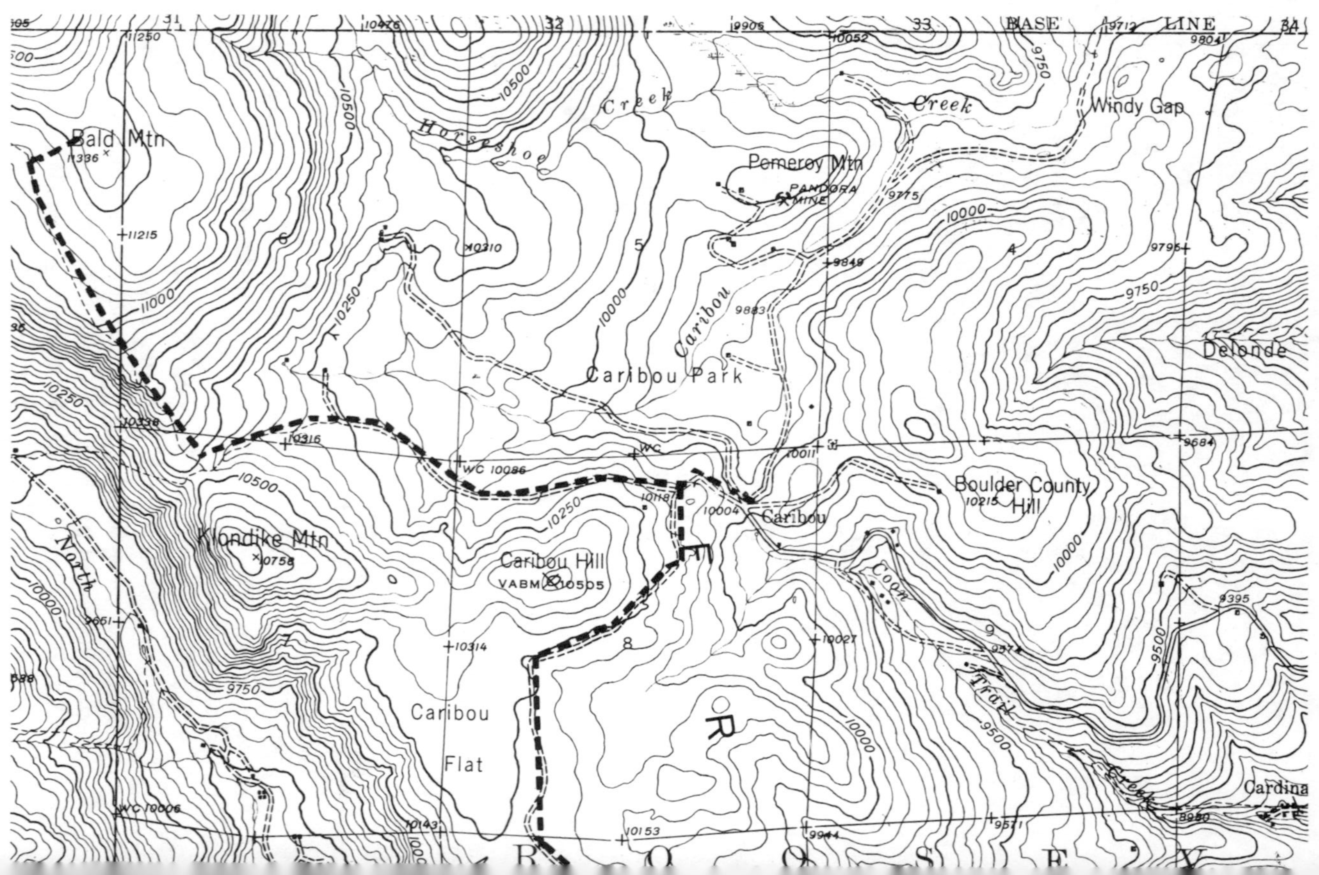
BASE LINE
Windy Gap
Creek
Pennsy Mtn
Delonde
Caribou Park
Caribou
Boulder County Hill
Bald Mtn
Klondike Mtn
Caribou Hill
VABM 10585
Caribou Flat
R
Cardinal

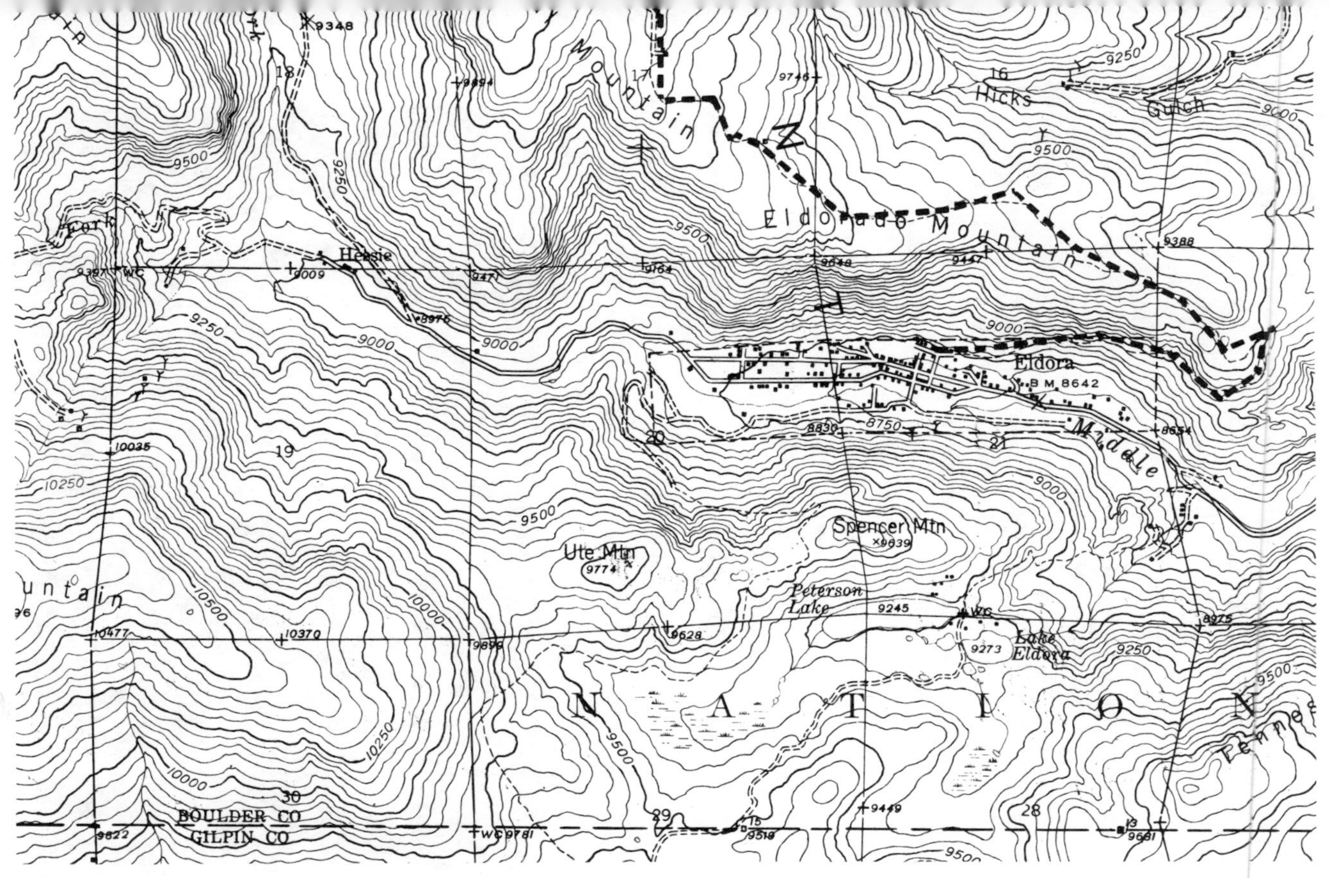

Mountain
Hicks
Gulch
Eldorado Mountain
9388
Hessie
Fork
Eldora
B M 8642
Middle
Spencer Mtn
9639
Ute Mtn
9774
Peterson
Lake
9245
Lake
Eldora
9273
N A T I O N
Tenner
BOULDER CO
GILPIN CO
9500
9250
9000
10000
10250
10500
10035
10370
10477
9628
9449
N

The Caribou Mine was the richest one in the area, and in 1882, silver from the mine was used to pave a street in Central City. When President U.S. Grant visited Central City, he was able to step out of his carriage onto this silver path, laid especially for the occasion.

The town was wiped out twice by fire, once in 1879, and again in 1905. By then silver mining was declining because of the low price, and the town never recovered.

Along with the silver, the Caribou area sits on an iron dike, making it quite an attraction for summer electrical storms.

Because of its location, the area generally has snow for at least nine months of the year, and a pretty constant west wind.

Hiking in the area offers a couple of possibilities:

a. Park by the sign. Hike along the jeep road going uphill to the south. This trail can be followed all the way to Caribou Flat which is also accessible from the town of Eldora. If desired, you could hike all the way over to Eldora, but you might wish to consider a car key exchange for this hike.

Distance to Eldora from Caribou: approximately 6 miles

b. Hike along the jeep road heading west. Upon reaching a fork in the road, turn right and head uphill to the north to climb

Ruins of the old mining town of Caribou

Bald Mountain. The trail has one short, steep pitch, but otherwise
is a gradual climb of 1,332 feet. Once you're above timberline,
you can see the old mine shack on the peak, and use this as a land-
mark when the trail peters out.

Distance up Bald Mountain: 3 miles
Elevation gain: 1,332 feet

Eldorado Springs

Eldorado Canyon Trail: Since you are hiking in a state park,
admission is charged. In 1988, if you parked at the entrance and
walked in, the fee was $1.00. If you drove into the park, you were
charged $3.00.

If you drive in to the trail, you'll be on a narrow, fairly rugged
road that ends up at a picnic area after .7 mile. As you drive along
the road, watch for technical rock climbers on the rock slabs. You
can either park in the picnic area and take the small trail north
of you to the trailhead, or park on the right side of the bridge east
of the picnic area and hike up the dirt road that is only open to
authorized vehicles.

The trail heads uphill on the right side of the road and climbs
steeply to the north. It has many switchbacks as it climbs up, levels
out, and then climbs up some more to reach a magnificent view
of the back range.

Distance to overlook: 3 miles

You'll soon drop down into the Walker Ranch property. A car
key exchange might be a good way to avoid going back up from
Walker Ranch to return to your car.

Distance: 5.5 miles
Elevation gain: 1,000 feet
Difficulty: Strenuous

Hotel Ruins: For a shorter hike, go up to the hold hotel ruins
via Rattlesnake Gulch Trail. The hike begins approximately .5 mile
up the dirt road from the parking area on the south side of the
road. It's marked with a wooden signboard map of the area.

The trail begins gently and then begins to climb through the
forest via some scenic switchbacks.

The view of the Continental Divide at the hotel ruin overlook
is well worth the hike. The hotel itself has almost disappeared.

The trail has two forks going to the south which go up to the railroad tracks, but neither is marked by signs. However, both have rock cairns along the left side of the trail. The top one comes just before the overlook and ruins and has an arrow constructed of rock pointing back to the south. This trail is narrow, but easy enough to follow up to the tracks where the train enters a tunnel.

Distance: Hotel ruins: 1.9 miles; overlook of Continental Divide: 3.1 miles
Elevation gain: 1,650 feet
Difficulty: Easy

Boulder Open Space

Boulder has made some large open space purchases as a result of the money obtained from a .4 percent sales tax originally approved in 1967. Now the city owns 17,268 acres, and has spent many hours in establishing trails, trailheads, and picnic facilities. Currently, Boulder owns land which rings the city and extends both into the mountains as well as farmland and ranches to the east. I've found that fall and spring are the best times to enjoy the plains areas since very little shade is available.

Flatirons Vista: Doudy Draw Trail's southern end begins from Highway 93, 6 miles south of Boulder and .3 mile past the intersection of Highways 93 and 128. A road heads to the west from the parking lot, gradually narrowing to become a trail which contours down to cross a creek. Cattle graze all along here, so be sure to close all gates behind you.

Distance to here: 1.9 miles
Elevation gain: 400 feet
Difficulty: Easy

The trail then intersects Community Ditch Trail. From this point, you can either follow Community Ditch to its intersection with Highway 93, or take the Doudy Trail southwest to its northern end by the Eldorado Springs Road. A car key exchange would work well for this hike.

Distance one way for Doudy Draw: 2.3 miles
Distance for Community Ditch: 1.1 miles to Highway 93

Doudy Draw Trailhead at Flatirons Vista

Marshall Mesa: The Marshall area was mined in the 1800s, and in 1870, a spark from a campfire ignited a vein of coal at the back of one of the caves, setting the coal seam on fire. The fire continues to burn and in places the ground surface temperature reaches 300 degrees F. You may be able to see the smoke from this smoldering fire as you reach the top of the mesa and look around you.

Also, while you're in the area, you may be able to spot some of the original powder caves that were even lived in by some of the early miners who were unable to afford any other housing. During 1910–1914, these slopes were used by soldiers who were posted there to protect "scabs" from the striking coal miners.

A newly constructed trail leaves the parking area on Highway 170 a short distance southeast of Marshall. This trail, heading southwest, connects with Community Ditch after 1.2 miles. At this point, you can hike west on Community Ditch Trail to Highway 93, and to extend your hike, cross Highway 93 to pick up the extension of Community Ditch and hike to its intersection with Doudy Draw Trail. Follow Doudy Draw to its termination on the Eldorado Springs Road.

Distance: approximately 3 miles one way
Elevation gain: 300 feet
Difficulty: Easy

Another option is to hike Marshall Mesa to Community Ditch, which then intersects the Greenbelt Plateau Trail. Hike south for 1.6 miles to its end at the parking lot off Highways 128 and 93.

Distance: approximately 3 miles one way

If you follow Community Ditch Trail to the east, it will end after a mile near a lake, which is privately owned.

The trail across the Marshall Mesa follows Community Ditch.

Sawhill and Walden Ponds Wildlife Habitats: These 15 ponds are located 9 miles east of Boulder. Drive east out Baseline Road to 75th and turn left. Head north, and after passing Jay Road, begin watching for the turn-off to the west approximately 1 mile farther.

Boulder Creek's ancient floodplain once covered this area, leaving behind much sand and gravel. The gravel was mined from the area for almost twenty years, finally ending in the 1970s. Mining still goes on in nearby areas. Following the mining, the ponds were left to become a wildlife habitat.

Senior citizens fish in the largest of the ponds.

The cottonwoods on the west side of the pools are just a few left behind from the many that once lined Boulder Creek. These form an ideal spot for many native shrubs, grasses, and nocturnal animals such as coyotes, rabbits, raccoons, owls, skunk, squirrel, and fox.

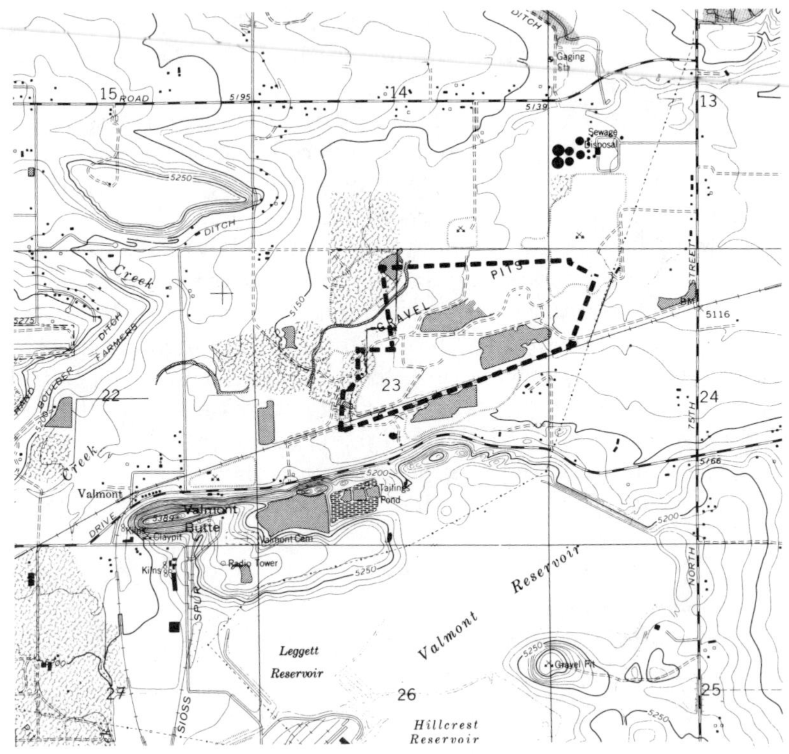

Bird watchers thoroughly enjoy these ponds since Colorado is located midway between the northern and southern breeding grounds of many waterfowl. You'll see many ducks on the ponds, both dabblers and divers. The dabblers, including mallards and teals, feed on the surface of the water, or on plants growing just beneath the water's surface. They feed by tipping over, with their tails held high in the air. The divers, whose legs are closer to their tails, dive beneath the water for their food.

The ponds have a self-guiding nature trail with signposts around some of the lakes. There were pamphlets available at one time, but these are now out of print.

Rabbit Mountain

Rabbit Mountain is located 15 miles north of Boulder. To reach it, drive north on Highway 36 to Lyons. Turn east on Highway 66 and continue east for 1.1 miles. Watch for the large orange water

127

storage tank on the north side of the road. This is N. 53rd. Turn left and continue north on this unpaved road for 2 more miles to reach the parking lot.

The park has 3 miles of trails. The most obvious one is the road that heads off to the right, circling the ridge. As you come around on the north side of the ridge, you get a good overlook of the small lakes and the eastern plains beyond.

In 1988, when I checked the area out, I followed another faint road that continued to go around the north side of the second knob, and seemed to return to the south to where I had parked. However, this road soon petered out into a faint trail, and then I was bush-whacking my way down a very steep hillside. As long as I stayed on the left side of the ravine, I was able to pick up the trail occa-sionally, but the going was rough. I would encourage you to retrace your path back via the road you followed up.

You can also climb up to the ridge on the left side of the park-ing lot.

There are rattlesnakes in the area, so be on the lookout.

Distance: loop, 3 miles
Elevation gain: 2,500 feet
Difficulty: Easy

Cottonwood Trail

To reach this trail, drive out the Longmont Diagonal from Boulder, passing under the 47th Street overpass to Independence Road. Turn right, and watch for the parking area a short distance to the east. In 1988, the concrete bikepath south of the parking lot dead-ended after about a half mile.

The trail itself is on the north side of the road and east of the parking lot. It passes many old cottonwood trees, which are espe-cially beautiful in the fall. It dead-ends near the Diagonal.

Distance: 1.2 miles one way
Difficulty: Easy

Wonderland Lake Trail

To reach this trail, drive out Linden to Wonderland Hill. Turn right and park by the bikepath on the north side of the road at the intersection of Linden Park and Wonderland Hill.

This bikepath offers you two options for circling the lake. You can either go around from the east side or the west side.

If you hike around the west side, you'll see a trail continuing up a steep hill to the north. Upon cresting the hill, you'll see an old road that continues north.

After about a mile, you'll reach an intersection on this road, with one spur continuing northwest. This spur will come out on Lee Hill Road. The trail also circles around the knob to the west to rejoin the road you hiked originally. However, all the land to the west of the trail isn't open space property, so watch for private property markers.

If you hike the fork to the right, you'll also come out on Lee Hill Road.

Distance to Lee Hill Road: 3.8 miles
Difficulty: Easy

In 1988, the open space map indicated that another trail continued to the north on the north side of Lee Hill Road. However, this wasn't in place yet, and plans for the development of the land going north to Beech were still indefinite.

Rock Creek Farm

Rock Creek Farm is located 9.4 miles east of Boulder on Dillon Road, or 1 mile northwest of Broomfield on S. 104th. This farm offers you an 8-mile corridor around the farm. The trail has many prairie dog holes along it. The late afternoon I checked it out, I also saw a beautiful red fox and several rabbits.

The trail goes around Stearns Lake and continues south to another parking area. From the second parking lot, you can hike along the perimeter of the farm and loop back around to return to the second parking lot.

Distance from lot to lot: 2 miles
Difficulty: Easy

A third trail is still being negotiated, which will run to the east toward Highway 287 outside of Broomfield, but it wasn't completed in 1988.

Boulder Creek Bikepath

This path has become one of Boulder's favorites, used by hikers, bikers, joggers, roller skaters, parents with strollers, and people of all ages.

Several easy entries with good parking include one at the western end of the trail at Eben Fine Park at 4th and Arapahoe, the Justice Center on 6th and Canyon, or at the library at 9th and Canyon. Parking is also available near the Clarion Hotel on 28th south of Arapahoe.

This paved path follows Boulder Creek from Eben Fine Park to 55th and Pearl, crossing under all the major street intersections, so you'll never have to deal with traffic. Watch for the fish viewing area at 28th Street near the Clarion.

Picnic tables are scattered along the route, and there are others at Eben Fine Park and at Scott Carpenter Park on 30th Street.

The kids' pond near the Justice Center is a great favorite with the younger generation.

Distance: 4.7 miles one way
Difficulty: Easy

South Boulder Creek Trail

Park in the lot on Baseline Road just before it joins Cherryvale Road. This dirt trail heads south beside South Boulder Creek, passes under the turnpike, and continues south to where it dead-ends near Marshall. Once you cross under the turnpike, you'll be on a gravel road that parallels South Boulder Road. Hike west for .2 mile, watching for the continuation of the path on the south side of the road.

Distance: 1.4 miles to the underpass; 2.3 miles to the southern end

Four Mile Canyon Creek Trail

This trail is reached by driving north out Broadway to Lee Hill Road. Turn left and drive west on Lee Hill for 1.1 miles. Turn left onto the dirt road which is unmarked except for a sign in 1988 for Carriage Hills Estates and Bow Mountain subdivision.

Drive for another 1.1 miles to Pinto Drive, also unmarked in 1988. The open space area wasn't marked yet, and there was no parking lot, so you'll need to park alongside the road near the long row of mailboxes on the south side of the road. The trail begins at the west end of Pinto, and is a real jewel.

Hike along the scenic stream bed that winds up the canyon. The trail climbs gently at first before going up and down some fairly steep hills. It dead-ends at some private property.

In 1988, the rangers had discussed the possibility of closing the trail due to its heavy use by mountain bikes.

Distance to end of trail: 1.75 miles
Elevation gain: 200 feet
Difficulty: Easy

Boulder Valley Ranch

Boulder Valley Ranch is located on Highway 36 approximately 1 mile from the intersection at 28th and Broadway. The open space available for hiking here is a shared area among hikers, mountain biking, and equestrians. The trails from the west end of the property pass through wide open fields.

One possibility for a hike begins south of the riding stables off the Foothills Highway on Hidden Valley Trail which joins the Mesa Reservoir Loop Trail. You can circle the reservoir and return to your starting point via Broken Arrow Trail, which rejoins the Mesa Reservoir Trail.

Another option is to begin from Hidden Valley and hike down to Mesa Reservoir, where you can pick up Broken Arrow Trail. This trail climbs to intersect Eagle Trail, which exits on the Boulder Reservoir Road 2.4 miles from the Longmont Diagonal.

The property is also laced with other trails that you can explore, but you will be sharing them with horses, so watch your footing.

Greenbelt Plateau

This trailhead is located off the intersection of Highways 128 and 93 on the northeast corner. You can hike north along the mesa to drop down to rejoin Highway 93 after 1.6 miles. This trail also intersects Community Ditch Trail, which also drops down to join Highway 93. Community Ditch Trail also takes you northeast to meet the Marshall Mesa Trail. If you hike down to the end of Marshall Mesa, your hike is approximately 2.8 miles.

Distance: 1.6 miles to Highway 93; 2.8 miles to Marshall Mesa
Difficulty: Easy

East Boulder Trail/White Rocks

This farmland is located off Arapahoe, east of 75th Street. It's on the north side of the street. Drive in on the dirt road .5 mile to the trailhead. This trail passes Teller Lake and loops through the farmland, passing Teller Lake #5 and eventually dead-ending at 95th Street.

Fishing is permitted in the lake. The shoreline is designated as a wildlife preserve, so no swimming or wading is permitted. You can also picnic by the south parking lot off Arapahoe.

Distance: 2.2 miles one way
Difficulty: Easy

Summary of Trails

Trail	Distance From Boulder (in mi.)	Elevation Gain (in ft.)	Length of Trip, One Way (approximate, in mi.)	U.S. Geol. Survey Maps
Allenspark Area				
Meadow Mountain	28	2,800	4.0	Allenspark
St. Vrain Mountain	28	3,332	5.5	Allenspark
Arapaho Pass Knob	22	1,676	3.8	Monarch Lake
Sunshine Canyon				
Bald Mountain Scenic Area	4.3	200	.50	Boulder
Betasso Preserve	6.2			
Bummer's Rock		270	.5	Boulder
Canyon Trail		400 (lost and regained)	2.9	Boulder
Boulder Mountain Parks				
Mesa Trail		600	6.0	Boulder, Eldorado Springs
Woods Quarry		250	.4	Boulder
NCAR		80	.5	Boulder
Enchanted Mesa		400	1.2	Boulder
McClintock Nature		400	.7	Boulder
South Boulder Creek	1.1	200	2	Eldorado Springs
Big Bluestem	1.1	500	2.3 .8	Eldorado Springs
South Shanahan	0	640	1.9	Eldorado Springs
North Shanahan	0	640	1.3	Eldorado Springs
Skunk Canyon	0	530	.7	Eldorado Springs
People's Trail	0	500	2.0	Eldorado Springs
Four Pines	0	500	.5	Eldorado Springs
Bluebell-Mesa	0	300	.5	Eldorado Springs
First Flatiron	0	800	.6	Eldorado Springs
Second Flatiron	0	800	.5	Eldorado Springs
Bluebird-Baird		300	.8	Boulder
Chautauqua		280	.6	Boulder
Mallory Cave		700	.4	Boulder
Bear Cave		400	1.0	Boulder
Harmon Cave		400	.25	Boulder
Royal Arch		1,000	.9	Boulder
Bear Peak via Bear Canyon		2,200	3.2	Boulder
Bear Peak via Fern Canyon		2,100	1.3	Boulder
Bear Peak via Shadow Canyon		2,100	1.7	Boulder
Flagstaff		1,050	1.5	Boulder
Boy Scout		80	.6	Boulder
May's Point		80	.2	Boulder
Artist Point		40	.1	Boulder

Tenderfoot		1,000	1.5	Boulder
Ute		160	.5	Boulder
Plains Overlook		40	.3	Boulder
Range View		160	.5	Boulder
Gregory Canyon		800	1.2	Boulder
Saddle Rock		1,200	1.0	Boulder
Amphitheater		550	.5	Boulder
Greenman		1,500	1.5	Boulder
Ranger		1,450	2.3	Boulder
West Ridge		600	1.5	Boulder
Long Canyon		750	1.5	Boulder
Mount Sanitas		1,200	1.2	Boulder
Red Rocks		400	.5	Boulder
Aqueduct Trail		400	2.0	Boulder
Mt. Sanitas Valley		200	1.5	Boulder
Boulder Open Space				
Doudy Draw	5	−400	2.3	
Community Ditch	4	0	1.1	
Marshall Mesa	2.5	200	1.2	
Greenbelt Plateau	5	0	1.6	
Rabbit Mountain	15	2,500	3.0	
Cottonwood	6.5	0	1.2	
Wonderland Lake	0	200	3.8	
Rock Creek Farm	9.4	0	2	
Boulder Creek Bikepath	0	0	4.7	
Four Mile Canyon Creek	2.2	200	1.75	
Boulder Valley Ranch	1	0	varied	
Greenbelt Plateau	5	0	1.6	
East Boulder-White Rocks	7	0	2.2	
Caribou-Bald Mountain	22.3	1,332	3.0	Nederland
Caribou-Eldora	22.3		6.0	Nederland
Eldorado Ski Area	21			
Bryan Mountain		1,523 via Cannonball 1,850 via Jenny	2.5	East Portal, Nederland
Guinn Mountain		1,807 via Jenny	4.0	
Town of Eldora	24			
Mineral Mountain		1,291	3.0	Nederland
Eldorado Mountain		1,019	2.0	
Caribou Hill		1,861	5.5	
Klondike		2,129	6.0	
Spencer		800	2.0	
Eldorado Springs-Hotel Ruins	6	1,650	1.9	
Eldorado Springs-Walker Ranch	6	1,000	4.5	
East Portal	26			
Jasper Lake-King Lake		3,000	15.0 (round trip)	Nederland, East Portal

Jenny Lind Gulch- Jumbo Mountain		1,165	4.0	Nederland
Golden Gate Park				
Black Bear		1,000	1.1	Black Hawk, Tungsten
Horseshoe		800	2.3	
Buffalo		1,000	3.0	
Burro		400	3.4	
Blue Grouse		1,134	2.3	
Ground Squirrel		800	2.0	
Mule Deer		1,000	3.0	
Elk Trail		1,000	3.0	
Coyote		1,313	2.2	
Raccoon		200	1.3	
Snowshoe Hare		400	2.0	
Mountain Lion		1,110	5.9	
Eagle		400	2.1	
Left Hand Canyon				
Public Access	14	700	3.7	Boulder
Nugget Hill	14	1,362	2.5	Boulder
Shoshoni and				
Pawnee Peaks	30.5			Ward
Shoshoni		2,622	4.7	
Pawnee		2,598	4.2	
Switzerland Trail				
of America	10			
Sugarloaf to Glacier Lake			5.5	Gold Hill, Ward
Sugarloaf to Sunset			4.0	
Gold Hill to Sunset			4.0	
Gold Hill to Left Hand Canyon			3.5	
Sunset to Glacier Lake			4.0	
Sunset to Sugarloaf			4.0	
Glacier Lake to Sunset			9.5	
Sugarloaf Mountain	10	476	1.0	Gold Hill
Thorodin Mountain	19	1,500	3.0	Tungsten
Upper Forest Lake **via Jenny Creek**	24	1,727	6.5	Nederland, East Portal
Walker Ranch	7.4			
S. Boulder Creek		− 560	1.0	Eldorado Springs
Meyers Homestead		600	2.5	
Crescent Meadows		400	1.5	
Columbine		400	2.5	
Eldorado Canyon		920	5.5	
Loop		− 560 + 400	8	
White Ranch	25.2			
Rawhide		− 400	4.2	Ralston Butte
Wranglers Run		0	.8	
Waterhole		200	.6	

Belcher Hill	1,000	2.5
Mustang	600	2.3
Sawmill	50	.6
Maverick	280	.9
Longhorn	600	2.7